My Italian Kitchen

Home-Style Recipes Made Lighter & Healthier

Janet Zappala

The Healthy Italian

Addicus Books
Omaha, Nebraska

My Italian Kitchen

Home-Style Recipes Made Lighter & Healthier

Janet Zappala

ISBN 978-1-886039-02-5

*Cover and interior design by Peri Poloni-Gabriel,
  Knockout Design, www.knockoutbooks.com*

Cover food styling by Betty Barlow

Cover photo by Paul Sirochman

*Page 51 photo by George Feder,
  Top Guns Photography*

Library of Congress Cataloging-in-Publication Data

Zappala, Janet
    My Italian kitchen : home-style recipes made lighter
    & healthier / Janet Zappala.
        p. cm.
    Includes index.
    ISBN 978-1-886039-02-5 (alk. paper)
    1. Cookery, Italian. I. Title.
    TX723.Z37 2010
    641.5945—dc22

                                        2009035951

Addicus Books, Inc.
P.O. Box 45327
Omaha, Nebraska 68145
www.AddicusBooks.com

Printed in the United States of America

10 9 8 7 6 5 4 3 2 1

In loving memory of my mother, who always knew how to stir things up.

Mary and Janet Zappala

Introduction

My love for food began at a very early age as I watched my mother create her own brand of memorable meals that were always made with care. When it came to cooking, she had a special touch — an innate sense of which ingredients worked best together. Perhaps it was because she had been cooking for her family of six since the age of nine!

Over the years, Mom fine-tuned her cooking into skills that she was proud of. More importantly, cooking allowed her to share countless meals with family and friends. When they knew Mary was cooking, they always found a way to gather around her kitchen table, and nothing made her happier.

It's those memories that continue to fuel my love for cooking. Every time I'm in the kitchen, I think of Mom. I remember the times we spent sharing laughs and endless meals, including some of my forever favorites — stuffed shells with homemade marinara sauce, Italian bread salad, lamb shanks, and stuffed artichokes. I especially remember the mornings she would make her sour-cream coffee cake—from scratch of course, I would wake up to the eye-opening aroma of the cake baking. To this day, it's still one of my favorite desserts.

Now, I'm pleased to share these recipes, mostly Italian of course, but with a few more of my favorites added because they are too tasty for me to not include in this book. I've re-created many of them so that they're more healthful, but without compromising their great taste. Chances are you're like me and love eating well without having to worry so much about what's in the food you're consuming. With my recipes, I've taken away the worry. These delicious dishes will have everyone saying, "Mmm, this is good!" and asking how you whipped up such tasty meals with so little effort. I hope you enjoy preparing and sharing these wonderful meals with those you care about, as much as I and my family have throughout the years. You'll make memories that will last a lifetime.

Wishing you *buona salute!*

Foreword

When Janet Zappala told me about her cookbook, I was taken back to the time I first met her and her mother. I was a new host of a cooking show on National Public Television, and Janet was the seasoned television pro I hoped to emulate. She was a television news anchor and reporter and had interviewed me. As time went on, we became friends. On many occasions when I would visit Janet, her mother, Mary, would be there, cooking. Janet and I were always drawn into the kitchen by the tantalizing aroma from Mary's meals; we'd watch as she prepared some of her incredible Italian dishes from scratch.

In *My Italian Kitchen*, Janet shares many of these recipes, but she has raised the bar, making them lighter and more nutritious. An exceptional cook, Janet is also a certified nutritional consultant, and knows how to make recipes more nutritious, without sacrificing taste. Her recipes are easy to make and call for ingredients you can buy at most any market. With this book, if you can read, you can cook…and boy, will you impress others with the results! Enjoy every mouthwatering dish.

Chef Christina Pirello

Host, *Christina Cooks*, PBS
Author, *Cooking the Whole Foods Way*
www.christinacooks.com

Soups and Starters

Butternut Squash and Potato Soup

French Onion Soup

Vegetarian Chili

Homemade Salsa with Oven-Baked Tortilla Chips

Pesto Cheese Loaf

Warm Artichoke and Asiago Cheese Dip

Lightly Fried Zucchini Chips

Stuffed Mushrooms

Avocado Spread

Homemade Cheese Ball

Warm Spinach and Cheese Dip

Hummus

Butternut Squash and Potato Soup

This smooth yet hearty soup is easy to prepare, but it will make you look like a super chef to those lucky enough to have some…and you thought you couldn't cook!

NUTRITIONAL NOTE

Squash is touted as a superfood. Every half cup has 5 grams of fiber and payloads of vitamins A and C.

NUTRITION FACTS

(Per serving)
Calories: 185
Total Fat: 9 gms
Sodium: 211 mgs
Carbohydrates: 30 gms
Protein: 11 gms
Fiber: 7 gms

PREP TIME: 25 minutes   **COOK TIME: 45 minutes**   Serves 4

1 medium butternut squash

2 baking potatoes, peeled and cut in chunks

½ medium yellow onion, diced

2 medium carrots, peeled and diced

2 medium celery stalks, diced

2 cloves garlic, crushed

1 32-ounce container low-sodium vegetable broth

1 teaspoon salt

1 teaspoon cracked black pepper

2 teaspoons extra-virgin olive oil

Cut off and discard the top and bottom of the squash. Peel the squash with a vegetable peeler. Cut lengthwise in half; scoop out and discard the seeds. Cut the squash into 1-inch pieces. Put the squash, potatoes, onion, carrots, celery, garlic, and broth into a large sauce pot over medium-high heat; bring to a boil (about 10 minutes). Reduce the heat to a simmer. Cook for about 35 minutes, gently stirring occasionally, until all the vegetables are tender. Using an immersion blender, blend vegetables until smooth; season the soup with salt and pepper. Ladle the soup into individual bowls, drizzle with olive oil (about ½ teaspoon each), and serve.

TIP: *You'll find locally grown squash from late summer through early spring. When time is tight, try fresh-cut, ready-to-go butternut squash from your supermarket. Although a bit more expensive, it's already peeled and diced for you. Frozen butternut squash also works well.*

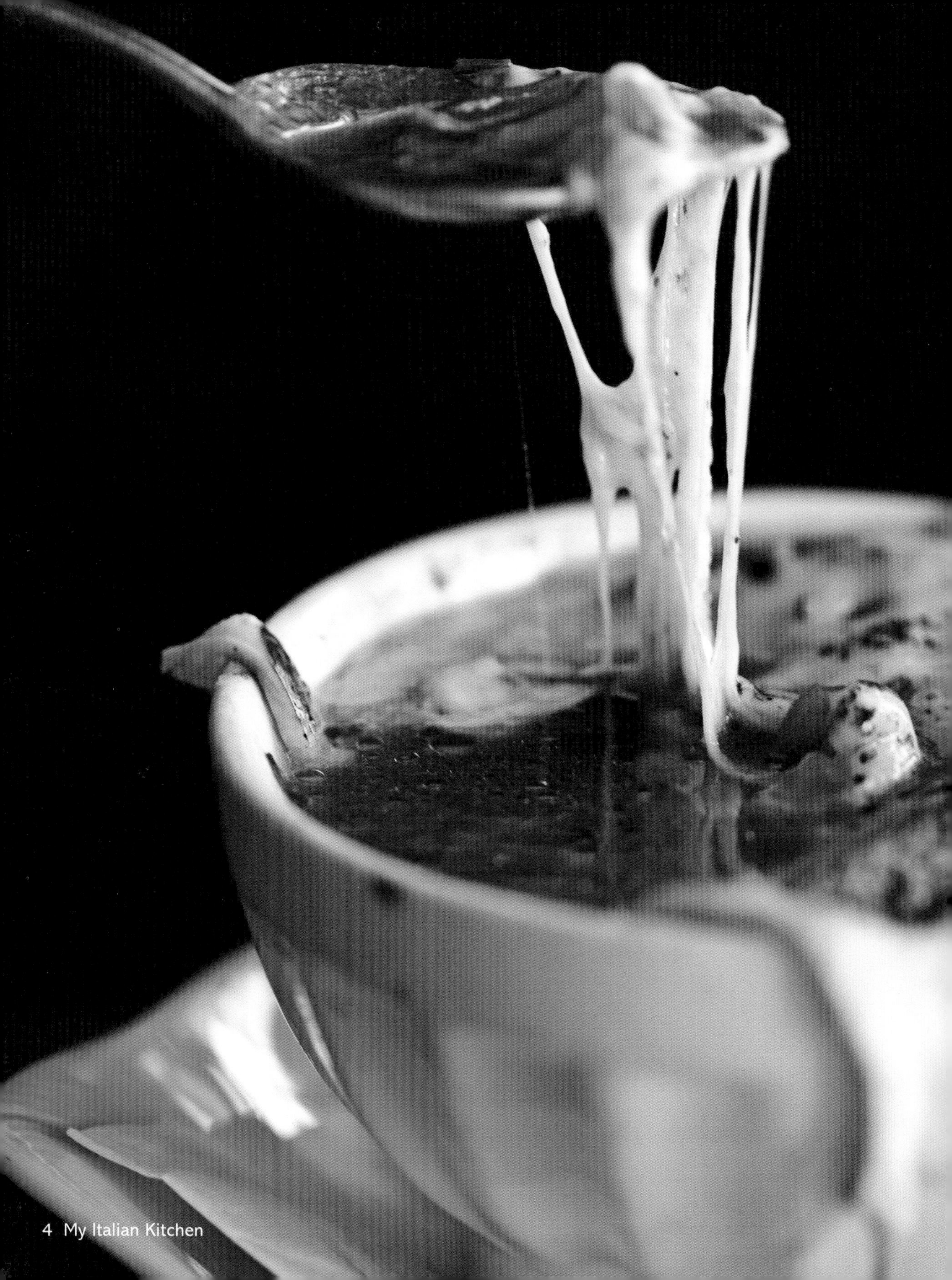

French Onion Soup

If you like onion soup, you'll love this recipe. It's lower in salt and fat than usual, but the classic taste of this favorite remains. If you have a hankering for the homemade version and you're into instant gratification, this one's for you.

PREP TIME: **15 minutes**	COOK TIME: **Approx. 40 minutes**	Serves 4

¼ cup extra-virgin olive oil

¼ cup natural buttery spread (such as Earth Balance or Smart Balance)

2 large yellow onions, sliced

1½ cups low-sodium chicken broth

1½ cups beef broth

3 cloves garlic, crushed

1 tablespoon low-sodium soy sauce

½ cup V8 juice

¼ cup port wine

1 teaspoon salt

1 teaspoon black pepper

4 slices whole-wheat baguette

4 slices reduced-fat Swiss cheese (such as Jarlsberg Lite)

NUTRITIONAL NOTE

Yellow onions are high in vitamin C, low in saturated fat, and a good source of fiber.

NUTRITION FACTS
(Per serving)
Calories: 193
Total Fat: 7.5 gms
Sodium: 488 mgs
Carbohydrates: 18 gms
Protein: 19.2 gms
Fiber: 3.2 gms

Heat the olive oil and butter alternative in a large sauce pot over medium heat for 1 minute. Add the onions; stir to combine. Sauté 5 minutes, stirring occasionally. Add the chicken and beef broths, garlic, and soy sauce. Stir thoroughly. Reduce the heat and simmer for 10 minutes.

Preheat the oven to 350°F. Increase the heat to medium, stir in the V8 juice, port wine, salt, and pepper. Bring to a boil. Reduce the heat and simmer for 20 minutes, stirring occasionally. While the soup is simmering, arrange the bread slices on a baking sheet; toast for 10

(recipe continues)

minutes. Remove the toast from the oven and turn the oven temperature to broil. Ladle soup into ovenproof bowls. Top each bowl with a slice of toast and a slice of cheese. Broil for 2 minutes or until the cheese melts. Serve immediately.

Vegetarian Chili

I make this chili throughout the year and at least once a week in winter. It's a deliciously satisfying dish that will warm you up and provide you with a bowlful of vitamins.

PREP TIME: **15 minutes**   COOK TIME: **40 minutes**   Serves 4-5

2 tablespoons extra-virgin olive oil

1 cup chopped carrots

1 cup chopped celery

1 cup diced yellow onion

3 cloves garlic, crushed

2 cups low-sodium vegetable broth

1 28-ounce can diced tomatoes, drained

1 8-ounce can tomato sauce

1 15-ounce can each, drained and rinsed well: pinto beans, red kidney

   beans, garbanzo beans (chickpeas)

1 teaspoon chili pepper or chili powder

1 tablespoon paprika

1 teaspoon salt

½ teaspoon black pepper

   Heat the olive oil in a large sauce pot over medium heat for 1 minute. Add the carrots, celery, onion, and garlic. Sauté 8-9 minutes, stirring occasionally. Stir in the vegetable broth, tomatoes, tomato sauce, beans, and seasonings. Mix thoroughly. Cover; cook for 30 minutes over low-medium heat, stirring occasionally. Taste-test the chili while it's cooking, adjusting seasoning as desired. Serve immediately in warm bowls along with hot, whole-grain rolls.

NUTRITIONAL NOTE

This "vitamin" chili is brimming with fiber, vitamins A and C, and the antioxidant lycopene.

NUTRITION FACTS

(Per serving)

Calories: 312

Total Fat: 7.3 gms

Sodium: 370 mgs

Carbohydrates: 48.3 gms

Protein: 22 gms

Fiber: 7 gms

Homemade Salsa with Oven-Baked Tortilla Chips

Countless companies make tortilla chips, but nothing beats the taste of these "homemade" crunchy morsels served with fresh salsa.

NUTRITIONAL NOTE

No matter how we slice them, tomatoes are good for us. They're an excellent source of vitamin C and the antioxidant lycopene.

NUTRITION FACTS

(Per serving)

Calories: 241

Total Fat: 13 gms

Sodium: 20 mgs

Carbohydrates: 28 gms

Protein: 7 gms

Fiber: 2.5 gms

PREP TIME: **15 minutes**	COOK TIME: **14 minutes**	Serves 4

BAKED TORTILLA CHIPS

10-12 yellow corn tortillas

1 tablespoon extra-virgin olive oil

¼ teaspoon salt

SALSA

3 ripe Roma tomatoes, chopped

½ cup chopped red onion

2 cloves whole garlic

½ jalapeno pepper, seeded

2 teaspoons chopped cilantro

1 tablespoon lime juice

1 tablespoon red wine vinegar

1 tablespoon extra-virgin olive oil

Salt to taste

FOR TORTILLA CHIPS: Preheat the oven to 350°F. Lightly brush the tops of the tortillas with olive oil. Cut them into strips lengthwise, then across, and place them in a single layer on 2 large baking sheets. Sprinkle the strips lightly with salt. Bake for 14 minutes.

FOR SALSA: Chop the tomatoes in a food processor for 5-10 seconds until they're sauce-like but with some texture. Transfer the tomatoes to a medium-size serving bowl. Chop the onion, garlic, pepper, and cilantro in a food processor for 5-10 seconds. Stir into the tomato mixture. In a separate small bowl, combine the lime juice, wine vinegar, olive oil, and salt; whisk thoroughly. Pour the lime juice mixture into the tomato mixture; stir until combined. Serve with the warm tortilla chips.

TIP: *For the tortillas, try the non-GMO (non–genetically modified organisms). They're all-natural and taste the same as conventional corn tortillas.*

Pesto Cheese Loaf

This loaf makes a delicious treat anytime, but it's especially handy for entertaining. Don't be surprised if your guests beg you for the recipe as my family's friends did. I had to wrestle this one away from Mom, who, I believe, had to wrestle it away from her friend Jeri. Serve the loaf with your favorite whole-grain crackers.

NUTRITIONAL NOTE

Basil contains high amounts of vitamin K, essential for healthy blood and bones. It's also a good source of fiber, vitamin C, and potassium.

NUTRITION FACTS

(Per serving)
Calories: 250
Total Fat: 14 gms
Sodium: 430 mgs
Carbohydrates: 15 gms
Protein: 16 gms
Fiber: 4.2 gms

PREP TIME: 30 minutes   Serves 8

5 ounces crumbled blue cheese, softened

2 8-ounce containers reduced-fat cream cheese, softened

1 cup raw spinach leaves, packed

¾ cup fresh parsley, packed

6-8 fresh basil leaves

1 small clove garlic

¼ cup extra-virgin olive oil

¼ cup pine nuts

1 cup freshly grated Parmesan cheese

¼ -½ cup sun-dried tomatoes, finely chopped

TO MAKE CHEESE MIXTURE: In a medium-size bowl, stir together the blue cheese and cream cheese until very spreadable; set it aside.

TO MAKE PESTO: In a food processor, combine the spinach, parsley, basil, and garlic. Slowly add the olive oil and pine nuts. Pulse until the nuts are roughly chopped. Spoon the pesto mixture into a medium-size bowl. Add the Parmesan and stir until thoroughly combined.

TO ASSEMBLE LOAF: Spread ⅓ of the cheese mixture on the bottom of an 8½ x 4½-inch glass loaf pan. Follow with a layer of pesto, then a sprinkle of sun-dried tomatoes. Repeat, making 4 layers in all, ending with a thin layer of cheese mixture on top. Serve immediately, or chill and serve later.

Warm Artichoke and Asiago Cheese Dip

I serve this when I want a really great-tasting dip that I can put together quickly. It's a guaranteed winner whenever family and friends visit.

PREP TIME: **8-10 minutes**	COOK TIME: **30 minutes**	Serves 4

1 9-ounce box frozen artichoke hearts, chopped into small pieces

¼ teaspoon black pepper

1 cup shaved Asiago cheese

½ cup grated Parmesan cheese

¼ cup light mayonnaise

Preheat the oven to 350°F. In a medium-size bowl, add the artichoke hearts, black pepper, and Asiago and Parmesan cheeses. Using your hands, toss lightly to combine. Add the mayonnaise; stir thoroughly. Spoon the mixture into a 1½-quart casserole dish. Bake for 30 minutes or until the dip begins to bubble slightly. Serve warm with your favorite whole-grain crackers.

NUTRITIONAL NOTE

A member of the sunflower family, the artichoke is rich in minerals, including magnesium, potassium, iron, and calcium.

NUTRITION FACTS

(Per serving)

Calories: 130

Total Fat: 6.75 gms

Sodium: 177 mgs

Carbohydrates: 10 gms

Protein: 6 gms

Fiber: 3 gms

Lightly Fried Zucchini Chips

*These chips flew off our plates when we were kids. Imagine that —
vegetables flying off a child's plate! This is a guiltless pleasure that
everyone can enjoy.*

NUTRITIONAL NOTE

Zucchini is a good
source of vitamin C
and fiber.

NUTRITION FACTS

(Per serving)
Calories: 249
Total Fat: 11.6 gms
Sodium: 350 mgs
Carbohydrates: 20.8 gms
Protein: 12 gms
Fiber: 3 gms

PREP TIME: **15 minutes**   COOK TIME: **6 minutes per batch**   Serves 4

2 medium zucchini with smooth, unblemished skins*

1½ cups Italian-style bread crumbs

½ cup grated Parmesan cheese

Salt and pepper to taste

3 eggs

3 teaspoons water

2 tablespoons extra-virgin olive oil, plus 2 tablespoons for
    sautéing each new batch

Locatelli cheese, small wedge for grating

Try to go organic and eat the skin — that's where most of the nutrients are.

Rinse zucchini under cold water; pat dry. Cut into ¼-inch-thick
slices. On a large plate, blend together the bread crumbs, Parmesan
cheese, salt, and pepper. Whisk together the eggs and water in a
medium-size bowl. Dredge the zucchini slices through the egg wash,
then through the bread-crumb mixture. Place the prepared zucchini on
a separate plate. Heat 2 tablespoons of olive oil in a large skillet over
medium heat for 2 minutes. Add the zucchini and cook until golden
brown, about 3 minutes on each side. Using a strainer, transfer the
zucchini from the skillet to a plate lined with a paper towel to absorb
excess oil. Sprinkle the chips with freshly grated Locatelli cheese.
Serve immediately.

TIP: *You can buy zucchini year-round, but it's at its peak in late spring. Since zucchini chips are best eaten hot, I usually serve them in batches. As soon as they come out of the skillet, I put them on a plate, sprinkle some grated cheese on top, serve, and start a new batch.*

Stuffed Mushrooms

This appetizer was a staple in our home every holiday. The fragrant aroma of the cooking mushrooms drew everyone to the kitchen to wait oh so patiently for this mouthwatering treat. Bet you can't eat just one!

PREP TIME: **20-25 minutes**   COOK TIME: **20 minutes**   Serves 4

⅓ cup extra-virgin olive oil, plus 1 teaspoon to coat baking sheet, plus a little to drizzle on top

12 medium-size cremini or white button mushrooms with stems

2 cloves garlic, minced

3 teaspoons fresh parsley, finely chopped

½ cup Italian-style bread crumbs

½ cup grated Parmesan cheese, plus 1 tablespoon

Salt and pepper to taste

Preheat the oven to 350°F. Lightly coat a medium-size baking sheet with 1 teaspoon of olive oil; set it aside. Using a damp paper towel, gently clean the mushrooms. Carefully cut the stems from the caps; chop the stems finely. Arrange caps, stem side up, on a cutting board. In a medium-size bowl, add the chopped stems, garlic, and parsley; mix with your hands. Add the bread crumbs, ½ cup of Parmesan cheese, ⅓ cup of olive oil, salt, and pepper. Combine all ingredients thoroughly (the mixture should stick together). Spoon the stuffing generously into the mushroom caps. Sprinkle them lightly with the remaining tablespoon of Parmesan cheese. Place the stuffed mushrooms on the prepared baking sheet. Drizzle a little olive oil over each mushroom. Bake for 20 minutes or until heated through. Serve immediately.

TIP: *A food processor makes this dish a snap to prep; or a good, sharp chef's knife will do.*

NUTRITIONAL NOTE
Mushrooms contain potassium, selenium, magnesium, and fiber and have zero fat.

NUTRITION FACTS
(Per serving)
Calories: 160
Total Fat: 10.8 gms
Sodium: 142 mgs
Carbohydrates: 10 gms
Protein: 12 gms
Fiber: 5 gms

Avocado Spread

This is one of the easiest and most healthful spreads you can make. In a few minutes, you transform ripe avocados into a delicious spread that you can enjoy on everything from chips to tacos. My personal favorite is on whole-wheat or egg 'n onion matzos (cracker-like flat bread), a great snack when you're in the mood for something light and nutritious.

NUTRITIONAL NOTE

Avocados contain healthful mono-unsaturated fats, the "good" fats that can help reduce "bad" cholesterol. They're also high in vitamin E. The lemon juice is a good source of vitamin C.

NUTRITION FACTS

(Per serving)

Calories: 50

Total Fat: 4.5 gms

Sodium: 144 mgs

Carbohydrates: 3 gms

Protein: 1 gm

Fiber: 3 gms

PREP TIME: **5 minutes**   Serves 4

2 large, ripe avocados

1 teaspoon garlic powder

½ teaspoon black pepper

1 teaspoon extra-virgin olive oil

½ teaspoon fresh lemon juice

Salt to taste

Rinse the avocados and cut them in half. Remove the pit from each. Scoop the avocado pulp onto a plate and mash it with a fork. Place the avocado in a medium-size bowl; add the garlic powder, black pepper, olive oil, and lemon juice. Mix thoroughly until smooth. Add salt to taste. Serve immediately.

TIP: *To remove the pit: Place the avocado on a cutting board. Using a large, sharp knife (keep your hands out of the way), strike the pit with the blade, twist, and lift. The pit should come right out.*

Homemade Cheese Ball

No matter who the "big cheese" is in your home, you'll all have a ball with this one. Grab your favorite whole-grain crackers and dig in!

NUTRITIONAL NOTE

Pecans are delicious and nutritious. They're high in protein and fiber and also contain essential nutrients including, thiamin, magnesium, and potassium.

NUTRITION FACTS

(Per serving)

Calories: 280

Total Fat: 20 gms

Sodium: 80 mgs

Carbohydrates: 8.5 gms

Protein: 19 gms

Fiber: 2 gms

PREP TIME: **5-10 minutes**   Serves 4

¼ cup finely ground pecans

2 heaping tablespoons low-fat cream cheese, softened

1 cup shredded extra-sharp Cheddar cheese

1 cup shredded reduced-fat Swiss cheese (such as Jarlsberg Lite)

½ teaspoon dried mustard

¼ teaspoon Worcestershire sauce

1 ¼ tablespoon horseradish sauce

½ teaspoon port wine

Spread the pecans on a plate; set it aside. In a medium-size bowl, mix all ingredients except the nuts until they are thoroughly combined. Shape the cheese into a ball and roll it in the nuts until the cheese ball is covered. Serve immediately, or refrigerate and serve later at room temperature.

TIP: *The horseradish sauce is much smoother and lighter tasting than straight horseradish, yet it still provides a little kick to keep things interesting.*

Warm Spinach and Cheese Dip

My close friend Georgeanne introduced me to this heavenly and healthful snack several years ago. It has been a favorite of mine ever since, especially for parties and on game-watching Sundays.

PREP TIME: **5 minutes**   COOK TIME: **5-6 minutes**   Serves 4

---

10 ounces frozen chopped spinach (in bag)

1 8-ounce container low-fat cream cheese, softened

1 cup sharp Cheddar cheese, shredded

1 tablespoon garlic powder

¼ teaspoon black pepper

Combine all ingredients in a microwave-safe 1½-quart casserole dish. Microwave on high for 5-6 minutes. Remove the dish from the microwave; stir the mixture until blended. Serve the dip warm with my Oven-Baked Tortilla Chips (*see page 8*).

NUTRITIONAL NOTE

Spinach offers an array of nutrients, including iron, calcium, and fiber.

NUTRITION FACTS
(Per serving)
Calories: 150
Total Fat: 7 gms
Sodium: 200 mgs
Carbohydrates: 5 gms
Protein: 13 gms
Fiber: 2 gms

Hummus

Hummus is a tasty spread made from garbanzo beans (chickpeas). It has been all the rage in the Mediterranean for ages and is nearly as popular here in the States. Homemade hummus served with warm flat bread or pita is a perfect pairing!

PREP TIME: **15 minutes**	COOK TIME: **2-3 minutes**	Serves 4

½ teaspoon extra-virgin olive oil, plus ½ cup extra-virgin olive oil

1 clove garlic, crushed

1 15-ounce can garbanzo beans, drained and rinsed well

Juice of 1 lemon

¼ teaspoon salt

¼ teaspoon black pepper

¼ teaspoon paprika

Parsley sprigs, for garnish

1 package Mediterranean flat bread, or whole-wheat pita bread, cut into triangles and heated

1 bunch green onions, cleaned and left whole

1 bunch small radishes, cleaned and left whole

Heat ½ teaspoon of olive oil in a small saucepan over medium heat for 1 minute. Add the garlic; sauté for 1-2 minutes or until golden. Remove from the heat. In a food processor, combine the garbanzo beans, ½ cup of olive oil, and cooked garlic; pulse on low speed for 20 seconds. Add the lemon juice, salt, and pepper; blend until creamy smooth. Transfer the hummus to a microwave-safe bowl and microwave on high for 20 seconds. Stir thoroughly. Sprinkle with the paprika, and garnish with the parsley. Serve with the warm bread of your choice and the onions and radishes.

NUTRITIONAL NOTE

When it comes to all-star cholesterol-lowering fiber foods, garbanzo beans lead the pack. They're a high-energy food and also help to balance blood sugar levels.

NUTRITION FACTS

(Per serving)

Calories: 60

Total Fat: 3.5 gms

Sodium: 85 mgs

Carbohydrates: 5 gms

Protein: 2 gms

Fiber: 5 gms

Salads

Panzanella (Italian Bread Salad)

Sliders and Slaw

Asian-Style Chicken Salad

Warm Spinach Salad

Watercress Salad with Capers,
Red Onions, and Blackberries

"Health Nut" Salad

Vine-on Tomato and Basil Salad

Panzanella (Italian Bread Salad)

With its sliced Tuscan bread, fresh basil, and tomatoes, this special dish is very popular among Italians. One tasty bite brings back happy memories of family eating around a big table and drinking Grandpa's homemade wine. Salute!

NUTRITIONAL NOTE

Bell peppers are an excellent source of vitamins C and A, and red bell peppers also contain the antioxidant lycopene.

NUTRITION FACTS

(Per serving)

Calories: 334

Total Fat: 22.5 gms

Sodium: 143 mgs

Carbohydrates: 43.9 gms

Protein: 26.5 gms

Fiber: 6 gms

PREP TIME: **20 minutes**	COOK TIME: **25 minutes**	Serves 4

SALAD

3 tablespoons extra virgin olive oil

1 each: red, yellow, and green bell peppers, roughly chopped

1 red onion, roughly chopped

4 plum tomatoes, quartered

4 cloves garlic, chopped

½ cup chopped fresh basil

Salt and pepper to taste

½ loaf day-old crusty whole-wheat baguette, cut into 1-inch cubes

DRESSING

½ cup extra-virgin olive oil

¼ cup red wine vinegar

1 shallot, minced

Salt and pepper to taste

FOR BREAD SALAD: Preheat the oven to 425°F. Lightly brush a large baking sheet and a medium size baking sheet with 1 tablespoon olive oil; set them aside. In a large bowl, combine the bell peppers, onion, tomatoes, garlic, and basil. Add 2 tablespoons of olive oil, salt, and pepper to the vegetable mixture. Using your hands, lightly toss all ingredients until they're coated.

Arrange the vegetable mixture on the large baking sheet in a single layer. Bake for 25 minutes or until the vegetables are roasted and browned.

While the vegetables are cooking, arrange the bread cubes in a single layer on the medium-size baking sheet. Put the bread in the oven during the last 10 minutes the vegetables are cooking. Toast the bread until golden (about 10 minutes), tossing occasionally to ensure an even color.

FOR DRESSING: Whisk together olive oil, red wine vinegar, shallot, salt, and pepper.

TO ASSEMBLE PANZANELLA SALAD: In a medium-size serving bowl, combine the cooked vegetable mixture and the toasted bread cubes. Pour the dressing evenly over the mixture as desired. Toss lightly to coat. Serve warm.

Sliders and Slaw

These mini-burgers come minus the bun. Paired with the cabbage slaw, they make a slider salad — a delicious and unique treat for lunch or dinner.

NUTRITIONAL NOTE

A cruciferous vegetable, napa cabbage contains selenium, vitamin C, and calcium.

NUTRITION FACTS

(For 2 sliders with slaw)
Calories: 415
Total Fat: 23 gms
Sodium: 357 mgs
Carbohydrates: 28.4 gms
Protein: 34 gms
Fiber: 5 gms

PREP TIME: **35-40 minutes**   COOK TIME: **Approx. 20 minutes**   Serves 4

SLIDERS

1 tablespoon extra-virgin olive oil, plus 1 tablespoon to brush on beet slices, plus 1-2 teaspoons for the 2 baking sheets

2 tablespoons finely chopped yellow onion

1 clove garlic, minced

¼ cup shredded carrot

1 pound lean ground beef, preferably organic or all-natural

1 egg white, whisked

¼ cup bread crumbs

2 teaspoons Dijon mustard

1 medium raw beet, peeled and thinly sliced

Salt and pepper to taste

GREEN CABBAGE SLAW

¼ pound fresh green beans, cut into thirds

¼ cup apple cider vinegar

3 tablespoons extra-virgin olive oil

1½ tablespoons honey

1 tablespoon dry mustard

Salt and pepper to taste

1 cup sliced radicchio

4 cups sliced napa cabbage

¼ cup sliced yellow onion

TO MAKE SLIDERS: Preheat the oven to 400°F. Lightly oil 2 medium size, nonstick baking sheets; set aside. Heat 1 tablespoon of olive oil in a medium-size saucepan over medium heat for 1 minute. Sauté the onion, garlic, and carrots until soft, about 2 minutes; let it cool.

In a medium-size bowl, combine the ground beef, onion mixture, egg white, bread crumbs, and Dijon mustard. Shape the meat mixture into about 10 small patties. Place the patties on one prepared baking sheet; refrigerate for 30 minutes. Place the beet slices on another prepared baking sheet. Brush beets lightly with olive oil, and season with salt and pepper; set them aside. Bake the beets for 15 minutes and the chilled patties for 12-15 minutes. To serve, place 2 beet slices on a plate, then 1 slider atop each beet. Top the slider generously with slaw.

TO MAKE SLAW: While the sliders are in the oven, boil the beans for 2-3 minutes to blanch. Transfer the beans from the cooking pot to a pot of cold water; set them aside. In a large bowl, whisk together the vinegar, olive oil, honey, dry mustard, salt, and pepper; set it aside. Drain the cooked beans and add to vinegar mixture, along with the radicchio, napa cabbage, and yellow onion. Using your hands, toss lightly to coat.

Asian-Style Chicken Salad

This is an updated version of a perennial favorite, one you'll be making again and again.

NUTRITION FACTS

(Per serving)

Calories: 217

Total Fat: 15 gms

Sodium: 300 mgs

Carbohydrates: 23 gms

Protein: 28 gms

Fiber: 6 gms

PREP TIME: 30 minutes	COOK TIME: Approx. 20 minutes	Serves 4

SALAD

4 medium carrots, shredded or cut thinly

1¼ cup snow peas

1 red bell pepper, cut into bite-size pieces

2 green onions, cut on a diagonal

1 11-ounce can mandarin oranges, drained

5 cups shredded napa cabbage

1½ pounds boneless, skinless chicken breasts, preferably organic
  or all-natural

1 tablespoon canola oil

¼ cup sliced almonds, toasted*

*To toast the almonds, place them on a baking sheet and bake for 5 minutes at 350°F. Remove from the oven; set them aside. Turn off oven.

DRESSING

2½ tablespoons light-brown sugar

1¼ teaspoon salt

1 teaspoon black pepper

2¼ tablespoons rice vinegar

1½ teaspoon low-sodium soy sauce

¾ cup canola oil

1½ teaspoons sesame oil

TO MAKE SALAD: In an extra-large salad bowl, combine the carrots, snow peas, bell pepper, scallions, mandarin oranges, and cabbage. Set it aside. Rinse the chicken under cold water; pat it dry. Cut the chicken on a diagonal into bite-size pieces. Heat the canola oil in a large skillet over medium heat for 1-2 minutes. Add the chicken. Cook about 12 minutes, turning the chicken every few minutes for even cooking. Remove the chicken from the heat; set it aside.

TO MAKE DRESSING: While the chicken is cooking, mix the sugar, salt, pepper, vinegar, and soy sauce in a small bowl. Slowly drizzle in the canola and sesame oils; whisk until thoroughly combined.

TO ASSEMBLE: Add the cooked chicken to the vegetables in the salad bowl. Add the dressing. Using your hands, toss the ingredients lightly to coat. Top with toasted almonds.

Warm Spinach Salad

The warm garlic-basil dressing really brings out the natural, nutty flavor of baby spinach and gives it a more tender texture. To enjoy this dish as a meal, toss in some leftover cooked chicken or shrimp.

NUTRITIONAL NOTE
Spinach contains calcium, iron, and vitamins A, C, and E.

NUTRITION FACTS
(Per serving)
Calories: 179
Total Fat: 10.83 gms
Sodium: 223 mgs
Carbohydrates: 7.1 gms
Protein: 11.8 gms
Fiber: 4 gms

PREP TIME: **20 minutes**   COOK TIME: **20 minutes**   Serves 4

SALAD

1 hard-boiled egg, chopped

1 5-ounce package fresh baby spinach, rinsed and dried

½ cup mandarin oranges, drained

½ cup red onion, sliced

½ cup pine nuts, toasted*

Salt and black pepper to taste

*To toast the pine nuts, place them on a baking sheet and bake for 6–8 minutes at 350° F. Remove from the oven. Turn off oven.

DRESSING

3 ounces extra-virgin olive oil

4 cloves garlic, minced

4-5 leaves fresh basil, torn (or 1 ½ teaspoons dried basil, crushed)

2 tablespoons red wine vinegar

TO COOK THE EGG: Remove an egg from the refrigerator and set it aside. Add warm water nearly to the top of a small saucepan; bring the water to a boil over high heat (about 6 minutes). Reduce the heat to medium. With a spoon, lower the egg into the water (the egg should be completely submerged); cook for 17 minutes. If the water boils too hard, the egg can crack or become rubbery. Reducing the heat will ensure that your egg cooks correctly. Transfer the cooked egg to a small bowl of cold water; let it sit for a few minutes before peeling.

TO MAKE SALAD: While the egg is cooking, place the spinach leaves into a large salad bowl. Add the oranges and onion slices.

TO MAKE DRESSING: Heat the olive oil in a small skillet over medium heat for 1 minute. Add the garlic and basil, sauté 2 minutes. Reduce the heat, and add the vinegar; cook for 3 more minutes.

TO ASSEMBLE: Pour the dressing over the spinach mixture. Add the chopped egg, pine nuts, salt, and pepper. Toss lightly to coat.

Watercress Salad with Capers, Red Onions, and Blackberries

This light, refreshing salad is simple to throw together. Just toss, serve, and indulge.

NUTRITIONAL NOTE

This salad features an array of nutrients. Watercress, which is a member of the cabbage family, is a very good source of vitamins B_1, B_2, and E. Blackberries are high in antioxidants and fiber, and a good source of potassium.

NUTRITION FACTS

(Per serving)

Calories: 102

Total Fat: 8 gms

Sodium: 60 mgs

Carbohydrates: 7.9 gms

Protein: 7 gms

Fiber: 5 gms

PREP TIME: **10 minutes**   Serves 4

2-3 bunches fresh watercress

1 tablespoon capers*

½ cup red onion, thinly sliced

½ cup fresh blackberries, larger ones cut in half

2 tablespoons extra-virgin olive oil

3 tablespoons fresh lemon juice

Salt and freshly ground black pepper to taste

Shaved Parmesan cheese (optional)

*Capers are pickled flower buds that are used as a garnish or, as in this recipe, a seasoning.

Rinse the watercress under cold water; pat it dry. On a cutting board, keeping each watercress bunch intact, cut off the root, discard, and trim about 2 inches off stems. Cut the bunch across into quarters. In a large salad bowl, toss together the watercress, capers, onion, and blackberries. Drizzle with the olive oil and lemon juice. Season with the salt and pepper. Using your hands, toss the salad lightly to coat. If desired, top with shaved Parmesan cheese.

"Health Nut" Salad

You can eat this salad to your heart's content because of its natural goodness. Top it with a few extra raspberries for a healthful and delicious dose of fiber and antioxidants.

PREP TIME: **10 minutes**   **Serves 4**

DRESSING

1 dozen fresh raspberries (if using frozen, thaw first)

¼ cup extra-virgin olive oil

¼ cup balsamic vinegar

1 clove garlic, minced

SALAD

½ pound spring mix, rinsed

½ cup dried cranberries

6 ounces crumbled goat cheese (mild is best)

¾ cup finely chopped radicchio (optional)

TO MAKE DRESSING: Gently rinse the fresh raspberries under cold water; pat them dry. Place the raspberries in a small bowl; mash them with a fork. Whisk in the olive oil, vinegar, and garlic until well blended. Set the mixture aside.

TO ASSEMBLE: Combine all salad ingredients in a large bowl. Drizzle the dressing on the salad, a little at a time. Toss lightly to coat. Taste-test and add more dressing as desired.

NUTRITIONAL NOTE

Aside from their wonderful taste, raspberries offer a wide array of health benefits, including antioxidants, which keep our cells healthy and help fend off damaging free radicals.

NUTRITION FACTS

(Per serving)
Calories: 270
Total Fat: 10.3 gms
Sodium: 44 mgs
Carbohydrates: 37 gms
Protein: 6.8 gms
Fiber: 5 gms

Vine-on Tomato and Basil Salad

Try this dish when you want a light salad without the greens. The best part will be dipping your favorite crusty bread into the dressing, or topping a slice of Italian bread with the tasty mixture, which is very much like bruschetta.

NUTRITIONAL NOTE

Tomatoes are a good source of fiber and the antioxidant lycopene, and they're off the charts in vitamin C.

NUTRITION FACTS

(Per serving)

Calories: 85

Total Fat: 6.6 gms

Sodium: 12 mgs

Carbohydrates: 6.5 gms

Protein: 2 gms

Fiber: 3 gms

PREP TIME: **10 minutes**   Serves 4

---

3 tablespoons red wine vinegar

1 clove garlic, crushed

6 fresh basil leaves, torn (or 1 teaspoon dried basil, crushed)

¼ cup extra-virgin olive oil

4 ripe vine-on tomatoes, chopped into bite-size pieces (Roma tomatoes also work well)

½ red onion, chopped

Salt and pepper to taste

In a medium-size bowl, stir together the vinegar, garlic, and basil. Slowly whisk in the olive oil, mixing thoroughly. Add the tomatoes, onion, salt, and pepper. Toss lightly to coat. Serve at room temperature.

TIP: *To get the best flavor, tomatoes should stay on the vine until they're fully ripened; then, remove vines before preparation. With their subtle, sweet taste, vine-on tomatoes work beautifully for this salad. They're available year-round and are at their peak from July through September.*

Pastas

Stuffed Shells Marinara

Mama Mia Ziti

Mom's Marinara Sauce

Creamy Tortellini with Fresh Peas
and Mushrooms

Pasta with Broccoli in Garlic
and Cheese Sauce

Cream of Pepper Pasta

Orzo Rainbow Pasta

Stuffed Shells Marinara

This special dish has been a family jewel for as long as I can remember. My grandmother and mother would have us kids help them stuff the shells, a chore we actually enjoyed. But of course, the best part was sitting down at the table and digging into these little treasures!

NUTRITIONAL NOTE

Enjoy the part-skim ricotta cheese—it has fewer calories and less fat, but still delivers when it comes to creamy and delicious.

NUTRITION FACTS

(Per serving)

Calories: 321

Total Fat: 10 gms

Sodium: 260 mgs

Carbohydrates: 32 gms

Protein: 20 gms

Fiber: 3 gms

PREP TIME: 30 minutes (for shells and sauce)

COOK TIME: Approx. 1 hour, 5 minutes (for shells and sauce)

Makes approx. 32 shells   Serves 4

1 12-ounce box jumbo pasta shells

1 15-ounce container part-skim ricotta cheese

2 eggs, lightly beaten

½ cup freshly grated Parmesan cheese

¼ cup chopped fresh basil

Salt and pepper to taste

Mom's Marinara Sauce *(see pg. 42)*

½ cup shredded mozzarella cheese

Preheat the oven to 350°F. Boil the shells for just 8 minutes. They will be a bit stiffer and easier to stuff than if they were fully cooked. While the shells are cooking, in a medium-size bowl stir together the ricotta, eggs, Parmesan cheese, basil, salt, and pepper until smooth and creamy. When the pasta is cooked, drain in a colander. Run the shells under cool water and drain again. Spoon a thin layer of marinara sauce on the bottom of a 13 x 9-inch baking dish. Fill each shell with the cheese mixture. Place the filled shells in the baking dish and top evenly but lightly with marinara sauce. Save any extra sauce for serving on the side. Cover the dish with foil and bake for 30 minutes. Remove the foil, sprinkle the mozzarella cheese evenly over the shells. Bake uncovered for 5 more minutes. Serve immediately.

Mama Mia Ziti

Sing it loud and sing it strong! Well, we may not have actually broken into song when Mom made her famous ziti, but we sure came close. One bite and you'll say (or sing) Mama Mia, too!

PREP TIME: **15 minutes**   COOK TIME: **Approx. 15 minutes**   Serves 4

---

1 pound box whole-wheat ziti

2 tablespoons extra-virgin olive oil

¾ pound cherry tomatoes, cut in half or 3 ripe Roma tomatoes,
    sliced into bite-sized pieces

2 large cloves garlic

1 teaspoon garlic powder

Salt and black pepper to taste

½ cup fresh basil leaves, torn

1 15-ounce container part-skim ricotta cheese

½ cup freshly grated Parmesan cheese

Cook the ziti according to package directions. Shortly before the pasta is done, heat the olive oil in an extra-large, deep skillet over medium heat for 1-2 minutes. Add the tomatoes, garlic, garlic powder, salt, and pepper; sauté for 3 minutes. Add fresh basil and sauté another 1-2 minutes; set aside. Drain the pasta with a small bowl under the colander to catch some cooking water. Add the pasta, ricotta, and Parmesan to the skillet; combine thoroughly. Add a little cooking water if needed for desired consistency. Serve immediately.

NUTRITIONAL NOTE

Whole-wheat pasta is a complex carbohydrate and is more nutrient rich than white pasta. If you can't make the leap just yet to whole wheat, at least try the enriched pastas. There are many options available.

NUTRITION FACTS

(Per serving)

Calories: 350

Total Fat: 8.5 gms

Sodium: 375 mgs

Carbohydrates: 48.3 gms

Protein: 28 gms

Fiber: 5 gms

Mom's Marinara Sauce

This pasta sauce defies description. I may be a bit partial because Mom made this a lot as we were growing up, and we loved it! But our family friends also went so wild over it that many would request a bowl of Mom's sauce without the pasta. It's that good!

NUTRITIONAL NOTE

Red sauces are more healthful than white because of their higher tomato content. Tomatoes are an excellent source of vitamin C and the antioxidant lycopene.

NUTRITION FACTS

(Per serving)
Calories: 141
Total Fat: 5 gms
Sodium: 157 mgs
Carbohydrates: 5 gms
Protein: 4 gms
Fiber: 2 gms

PREP TIME: **20 minutes**   COOK TIME: **Approx. 30-60 minutes**   Serves **4–6**

---

2 28-ounce cans of whole, peeled tomatoes, preferably
    Hunt's All-Natural, pureed*

2 15-ounce cans tomato sauce, preferably Hunt's All-Natural

1 tablespoon extra-virgin olive oil

2-3 cloves garlic, chopped

Small handful of fresh basil leaves, torn
    (or 1 ½ teaspoon dried basil, crushed)

1 teaspoon dried oregano

Salt and pepper to taste

¼ cup water, optional

*To puree tomatoes, put the whole, peeled tomatoes into a blender or food processor and puree for 5 seconds, leaving tiny chunks of tomatoes for texture.

Heat the olive oil in a large sauce pot over medium heat for 1 minute. Add the garlic and basil; sauté until the garlic turns golden. Add the pureed tomatoes, tomato sauce, oregano, salt, and pepper. Reduce the heat and stir; partially cover. Simmer for 30-60 minutes, stirring occasionally. If necessary, add the ¼ cup water about halfway through the cooking process and stir thoroughly. Serve with Stuffed Shells (*see page 38*) or your favorite pasta.

Creamy Tortellini with Fresh Peas and Mushrooms

I make this dish when I'm short on time but still want a really satisfying meal. It's easy and delicious. Serve with a salad, and dinner is done!

PREP TIME: **10 minutes**   COOK TIME: **10-12 minutes**   Serves 4

---

1 cup fresh green English peas or frozen petite peas

2 tablespoons extra-virgin olive oil

1 cup sliced fresh mushrooms

1 vegetable bouillon cube, crushed

2 cloves garlic, crushed

4 slices cooked ham, cut into small pieces

2 pounds tortellini, preferably tri-color

¾ cup heavy cream or 10 ounces evaporated fat-free milk

½ cup grated Parmesan cheese

Cracked black pepper to taste

Using a colander, rinse the fresh peas under cold water and drain. Bring a large pot of water to a boil for the tortellini. While the water is heating, heat the olive oil in a medium-size skillet over medium heat for 1 minute. Reduce the skillet heat to low; add the peas, mushrooms, bouillon cube, and garlic. Cook for 8-10 minutes, stirring occasionally. Add the ham at the last minute. When the pot of water comes to a boil, add the tortellini; cook according to package directions. Drain the tortellini and return it to the pot. Over low heat, stir in the cream. Add the cooked vegetable-and-ham mixture, Parmesan cheese, and black pepper; mix thoroughly. Serve immediately.

TIP: *This recipe works best with fresh or frozen peas, which retain their flavor longer and are lower in sodium than canned peas. When available, fresh English peas are perfect in this dish.*

NUTRITIONAL NOTE
Green peas are bursting with flavor and nutrients, especially fiber and protein. They also contain nutrients that help maintain bone health.

NUTRITION FACTS
(Per serving)
Using heavy cream
Calories: 357
Total Fat: 23 gms
Sodium 304 mgs
Carbohydrates: 28 gms
Protein: 31 gms
Fiber: 6.4 gms

Using evaporated fat-free milk
Calories: 332
Total Fat: 11.5 gms
Sodium: 304 mgs
Carbohydrates: 28 gms
Protein: 31 gms
Fiber: 6.4 gms

Pasta with Broccoli in Garlic and Cheese Sauce

This recipe has been in my family for many years, and it's no wonder — broccoli has its roots in Calabria, Italy, which is also where some of my family is from. (Coincidence? I think not.) It's a special favorite because of its simplicity and great taste.

NUTRITIONAL NOTE

Whole-wheat pasta has nearly 3 times more fiber than regular pasta. This not only fills you up faster, cutting down on your calorie intake, but it can also help to lower your risk of heart disease and diabetes. Enriched pasta is another healthful option. Broccoli, for its part, is rich in nutrients and contains more vitamin C than oranges.

NUTRITION FACTS

(Per serving)
Calories: 281
Total Fat: 8.7 gms
Sodium: 121 mgs
Carbohydrates: 44.9 gms
Protein: 12.5 gms
Fiber: 4 gms

PREP TIME: **15 minutes**   COOK TIME: **10-12 minutes**   Serves 4

---

1 pound fresh broccoli, or 1 16-ounce bag frozen broccoli florets

1 pound box whole-wheat or enriched pasta shells or spaghetti

2 cups water for the broccoli

$\frac{1}{3}$ cup extra-virgin olive oil

3 cloves garlic, minced

Salt and cracked black pepper to taste

1 $\frac{1}{2}$ cups freshly grated Parmesan or Locatelli cheese

Rinse broccoli under cold water; pat it dry. On a cutting board, chop the broccoli, including stems, into bite-size pieces; set it aside. Boil the pasta according to the package directions. While the pasta is cooking, in a medium-size sauce pot over medium heat, bring the 2 cups of water and broccoli to a boil. Reduce the heat, cover, and simmer 6-7 minutes for fresh broccoli. If using frozen broccoli, follow package directions. Either way, the broccoli should be a bright green color and fork-tender when done.

As the pasta cooks, heat the olive oil in a small skillet over medium heat for 2 minutes. Add the garlic; sauté until golden. Set it aside. Drain the pasta, placing a small bowl under the colander to reserve some cooking water. Return the pasta to the pot. Add the cooked broccoli, cooked garlic and oil, salt, and pepper. Mix in the grated cheese, tossing and stirring to combine. Add some reserved cooking water to the mixture to get desired consistency. Transfer the pasta to a large serving bowl. Serve immediately.

Cream of Pepper Pasta

I love this dish for its hint of red pepper taste, which makes it very different from basic marinara sauce. I call it my "saucy" sauce because of its bell-peppery kick.

PREP TIME: **10 minutes**   COOK TIME: **Approx. 40 minutes**   Serves 4

---

2 tablespoons extra-virgin olive oil

1 28-ounce can whole, peeled tomatoes

4 fresh red bell peppers, sliced

1 medium yellow onion, roughly chopped

6 fresh basil leaves, torn (or 1 teaspoon dried basil, crushed)

½ teaspoon salt

1 pound box penne pasta, preferably whole-wheat

¼ cup heavy cream

Heat the olive oil in a large sauce pot over medium heat for 1-2 minutes. Add the tomatoes, peppers, onion, basil, and salt. Cover, reduce heat to medium/low, and cook for 40 minutes, stirring occasionally. When the sauce is nearly done, boil water for pasta in a second large sauce pot. When the sauce is completely done, turn off the heat, stir and let it cool. Add the pasta to the pot of boiling water and cook according to package directions.

When the pasta is done, drain it, and return it to the same pot, cover. Using a ladle, transfer the sauce to a blender. On high, blend for 35-40 seconds until smooth. Return the sauce to the pot over low heat; stir in the cream. Add as much sauce as desired to the cooked pasta, and mix thoroughly. Serve immediately.

NUTRITIONAL NOTE

Whole-wheat pasta has fewer calories and more fiber than regular pasta and can be counted toward your daily whole-grain requirement.

NUTRITION FACTS

(Per serving)

Calories: 299

Total Fat: 8 gms

Sodium: 246 mgs

Carbohydrates: 52.6 gms

Protein: 17 gms

Fiber: 3 gms

Orzo Rainbow Pasta

When it comes to taste and health, this colorful pasta dish packs a powerful punch. It has a good amount of fiber and ingredients that go beautifully together — pasta, cheese, tomatoes, olive oil, and fresh basil. Mangia!

NUTRITIONAL NOTE

In addition to having fewer calories than regular pasta, whole wheat pasta also provides iron and important B vitamins.

NUTRITION FACTS

(Per serving)

Calories: 505

Total Fat: 23 gms

Sodium: 279 mgs

Carbohydrates: 59.8 gms

Protein: 25 gms

Fiber: 7 gms

PREP TIME: 20 minutes	COOK TIME: 8-10 minutes	Serves 4

1 pound box orzo pasta, preferably whole-wheat

½ cup red onion, finely diced

½ cup garbanzo beans (chickpeas), drained and rinsed

12 cherry tomatoes, rinsed and cut in half

1 heaping tablespoon fresh basil, chopped

½ cup pine nuts

3 cloves garlic, minced

½ cup extra-virgin olive oil

6-8 ounces mild low-fat goat cheese, softened and broken into small pieces

½ cup freshly grated Parmesan cheese

Salt and pepper to taste

Cook orzo pasta according to package directions; drain. In a large pasta bowl, combine warm orzo with remaining ingredients. Mix thoroughly and serve.

Janet serves up some of her favorites, including Orzo Rainbow Pasta, during a cooking demo at Philadelphia's La Cucina at the Market.

Fish, Meat, and Poultry

Baked Salmon with Lemon Dill Sauce

Blue Crab Linguine in Marinara Sauce

Seared Endive and Scallops in Citrus Vinaigrette

Fish Under Wraps

Mom's Memorable Meatballs

Crock Pot Roast

Teriyaki Steak

Sweet-and-Sour Sauce over Baby Back Ribs

Lamb Shanks over Orzo Pasta

Breaded Pork Chops Italiano

Spice 'Em Up Pork Chops

Mascarpone Stuffed Chicken with Marsala Date Sauce

Curry Chicken

Chicken in Light Beer Sauce

Roasted Lemon-Pepper Chicken

Turkey and Blue Cheese Burgers

Chicken Cutlets with Mushrooms and Mozzarella

Turkey Chili

Chicken Cacciatore

Baked Salmon with Lemon Dill Sauce

The American Heart Association recommends eating fish to help prevent heart disease. Salmon in particular has lots of heart-healthy essential fatty acids. Served with my Wilted Spinach (see page 89), this meal will be a boost to your good health.

(see page 89)

NUTRITIONAL NOTE

Try to opt for wild salmon versus farm-raised, as many studies have shown that farm-raised salmon contain 10 times more toxins than their wild counterparts do.

NUTRITION FACTS

(Per serving)
Calories: 104
Total Fat: 7.4 gms
Sodium: 63 mgs
Carbohydrates: 11.4 gms
Protein: 15.5 gms
Fiber: 0.4 gms

PREP TIME: **10 minutes**	COOK TIME: **12-18 minutes**	Serves 4

2 teaspoons extra-virgin olive oil

4 6-ounce wild salmon fillets

1 lemon, cut in half horizontally

¼ teaspoon fresh or dried dill weed

1 teaspoon fresh parsley, chopped fine (or ¼ teaspoon dried parsley flakes)

Salt and pepper to taste

LEMON-DILL SAUCE

½ cup nonfat plain yogurt

2 teaspoons fresh lemon juice

¼ teaspoon fresh or dried dill weed

Preheat the oven to 375°F. Brush a medium size baking sheet with 1 teaspoon of olive oil. Place the salmon fillets on the baking sheet. Brush the salmon lightly with the remaining teaspoon of olive oil. Squeeze the juice of ½ of the lemon over the fish; season the fillets with dill, parsley, salt, and pepper. Cut the remaining ½ lemon into thin slices; place the lemon slices on the fillets. Bake fish 12 minutes for medium-rare, longer if desired.

TO MAKE LEMON-DILL SAUCE: In a small bowl, whisk together all the lemon-dill sauce ingredients until they are thoroughly blended. Drizzle the sauce over the cooked salmon or serve it on the side.

Blue Crab Linguine in Marinara Sauce

The sweet, tender meat of the blue crab, combined with the marinara sauce, makes for a delectable dining experience. There isn't a lot of meat (about 2 ounces, depending on the size) in these tasty treats, but what there is of it is absolutely delicious. Have a nutcracker or a small mallet handy, and lots of napkins. This is one dish you can really sink your teeth into!

NUTRITIONAL NOTE

Crabmeat is an excellent source of protein. While somewhat high in cholesterol, it is very low in saturated fat, the main culprit in raising blood cholesterol levels.

NUTRITION FACTS

(Per serving)

Calories: 218

Total Fat: 6.6 gms

Sodium: 190 mgs

Carbohydrates: 25 gms

Protein: 18 gms

Fiber: 4 gms

PREP TIME: **10-15 minutes**   COOK TIME: **Approx. 40-60 minutes**   Serves 4

2 28-ounce cans whole, peeled tomatoes, preferably Hunt's All-Natural, pureed*

2 15-ounce cans tomato sauce, preferably Hunt's All-Natural

2 tablespoons extra-virgin olive oil

5 cloves garlic, chopped

¼ teaspoon dried basil

Salt and pepper to taste

¼ cup water, optional

1 pound linguine, preferably whole-wheat or enriched

8 whole blue crabs, fresh and cleaned, ready-to-cook

To puree tomatoes, put the whole, peeled tomatoes into a blender or food processor and puree for 5 seconds, leaving tiny chunks of tomato for texture.

TO MAKE MARINARA SAUCE: Heat the olive oil in an extra-large sauce pot over medium heat for 1 minute. Add the garlic; sauté until golden. Add the pureed tomatoes, tomato sauce, basil, salt, and pepper; stir thoroughly. Reduce the heat, partially cover, and simmer for 30-60 minutes, stirring occasionally. If necessary, add the ¼ cup of water about halfway through the cooking process.

TO COOK LINGUINE: While the sauce is simmering, cook the linguine according to package directions. When it's done, drain it, placing a small bowl under the colander to reserve some cooking water.

TO COOK WHOLE FRESH BLUE CRABS: While the sauce continues to simmer, toss whole crabs into an extra-large pot of boiling water, cook for 6 minutes.

TO ASSEMBLE: Remove crabs from pot and add to cooked sauce; gently stir to combine. Simmer the sauce over low heat 3-4 minutes until the crabs are thoroughly immersed in the sauce, adding some reserved water only if the sauce is too thick. Place the linguine, along with crabs and sauce, in a large serving dish. Serve immediately.

TIP: *During the warmer months, you can find some beautiful live blue crabs at your local seafood market. Also available are fresh, cleaned, ready-to-cook blue crabs, which are my choice.*

Seared Endive and Scallops in Citrus Vinaigrette

If you're fishing for a healthful food, scallops fit the bill. Their light taste makes them a good choice for lunch or dinner. But what sends this dish over the top is the dressing. Together, they're a perfect combination.

NUTRITIONAL NOTE

Scallops are high in protein, vitamin B$_{12}$, and potassium and low in calories, about 150 calories per 4-ounce serving.

NUTRITION FACTS

(Per serving)
Calories: 160
Total Fat: 5.4 gms
Sodium: 57 mgs
Carbohydrates: 18.3 gms
Protein: 11 gms
Fiber: 3 gms

PREP TIME: **15 minutes**   COOK TIME: **Approx. 15 minutes**   Serves 4

DRESSING

¼ cup honey

3 tablespoons Dijon mustard

2 tablespoons white wine vinegar

2 tablespoons orange juice

½ cup extra-virgin olive oil

2 shallots, minced

1½ tablespoons finely chopped cilantro

ENDIVE AND SCALLOPS

4 tablespoons extra-virgin olive oil

2 endive heads, leaves separated, rinsed and dried well

16 dry sea scallops (best for searing)

Salt and pepper to taste

3 tangerines or clementines, peeled and segmented,
    or 1 11-ounce can of mandarin oranges, drained

TO MAKE DRESSING: In a large bowl, whisk together the honey, mustard, vinegar, and orange juice. Whisk in the olive oil in a steady stream. Add the shallots and cilantro; mix to combine. Set it aside.

TO MAKE ENDIVE AND SCALLOPS: Preheat a large skillet on medium for 3 minutes. Using 2 tablespoons of the olive oil, brush the endive leaves and scallops. Lightly season the scallops with salt and pepper. Reduce the heat. Add 1 tablespoon of olive oil to the skillet. Add the endive; cook for 2-3 minutes on each side until the exterior turns golden brown. Remove the endive to a plate and cover to keep it warm. In the same skillet, over high heat, add the last tablespoon of olive oil; heat for 2 minutes. Add the scallops; sear for 2-3 minutes on each side (until a toasty brown color), making sure not to overcook them or they'll be chewy.

TO ASSEMBLE: Toss the scallops into the dressing, along with the tangerine or clementine segments; gently stir to combine. Arrange 4 scallops on each plate, add the endive, and drizzle dressing over each serving. Serve immediately.

Fish Under Wraps

This easy-to-prepare recipe is so delicious that even those who don't usually care for fish will enjoy it. When I made this for my youngest child, she said that for the first time she actually enjoyed eating fish! With this dish you'll never have to go fishing for compliments. (I had to say it.)

PREP TIME: **5 minutes**	COOK TIME: **20 minutes**	Serves 4

4 tablespoons extra-virgin olive oil

4 tilapia fillets

½ cup minced capers*

*Capers are pickled flower buds, and they add just the right touch of salty flavor to this crowd pleaser.

Preheat the oven to 390°F. Lay out 4, 14¾ x 12-inch sheets of aluminum foil. Spoon 1 tablespoon of olive oil on each sheet. Place a tilapia fillet on each sheet, turning to coat both sides of the fish with the oil. Spread minced capers on top of each fillet. Fold the foil over at the top and sides of each fillet to form an envelope, leaving a little room for the fish to "breathe." This will keep the steam in, which makes for a very moist and tender fish. Bake for 20 minutes. Serve the fish in the foil (fish will stay hot and covered in its flavorful juices).

NUTRITIONAL NOTE

Tilapia is a very good source of protein, selenium, and vitamin B12. Try to buy the more nutritious tilapia grown stateside, where the water they're farmed in is purified and recycled.

NUTRITION FACTS

(Per serving)
Calories: 93 (4 ounces)
Total Fat: 1.5 gms
Sodium: 37 mgs
Carbohydrates: 0 gms
Protein: 19.5 gms
Fiber: 1 gm

Mom's Memorable Meatballs

I remember coming home from school, opening the door, and smelling the inviting aroma of these meatballs. They were like a gift from Mom. Between us kids (and Dad) sneaking meatballs and dunking Italian bread into the sauce, it was a wonder we ever had any left for dinner. Try a few even without the sauce.

NUTRITIONAL NOTE

Organic meats contain no antibiotics or added hormones. The animals are also fed organic feed with no ground-up animal parts.

NUTRITION FACTS

(Per serving —three medium meatballs)

Calories: 200

Total Fat: 11 gms

Sodium: 380 mgs

Carbohydrates: 5 gms

Protein: 14 gms

Fiber: 6 gms

PREP TIME: **30 minutes**	COOK TIME: **1-2 hours**	Serves 5

MEATBALLS

¼ cup Italian-style bread crumbs

2 eggs, lightly beaten

¼ cup grated Parmesan cheese

¼ cup chopped fresh parsley

Pinch of salt and pepper

1½ pounds ground beef, pork, and veal (3-in-1 pack),
    preferably organic or all-natural

½ teaspoon water

1 tablespoon extra-virgin olive oil

SAUCE

1 tablespoon extra-virgin olive oil

½ cup chopped onion

3 cloves garlic, minced

2 28-ounce cans crushed tomatoes, preferably Hunt's All-Natural

2 15-ounce cans tomato sauce, preferably Hunt's All-Natural

½ teaspoon dried basil, crushed

½ teaspoon dried oregano, crushed

¼ cup water, optional

Salt and pepper to taste

TO MAKE MEATBALLS: In a large bowl, combine the bread crumbs, eggs, cheese, parsley, and a pinch of salt and pepper. Add the meat and ½ teaspoon of water; mix thoroughly. Shape the mixture into 15 medium-size meatballs. Heat 1 tablespoon of olive oil in a large sauce pot over medium heat for 1-2 minutes. Add the meatballs; brown them about 4 minutes on each side. Transfer the meatballs to a plate lined with a paper towel to soak up any excess oil.

TO MAKE SAUCE: In the same sauce pot, add 1 tablespoon of olive oil and the onion; sauté for 2 minutes. Add the garlic; sauté until golden. Stir in the crushed tomatoes, tomato sauce, basil, and oregano.

TO COOK: Add the meatballs to the sauce pot, gently stir, and bring to a boil. Lower heat; partially cover. Simmer 1-2 hours, stirring occasionally. Add the water if the sauce gets too thick. Taste-test and season with salt and pepper. Serve with your favorite pasta.

TIP: *You can make the meatballs smaller for a great party appetizer.*

Crock-Pot Roast

After one bite of this tender beef you won't be able to get enough of it. Every mouthful is a palate pleaser.

NUTRITIONAL NOTE

Garlic has many nutrients, including, iron, folate, calcium, and magnesium. It also helps to detoxify the body and keeps the immune system strong.

NUTRITION FACTS

(Per serving)
Calories: 170
Total Fat: 5 gms
Sodium: 155 mgs
Carbohydrates: 11 gms
Protein: 19 gms
Fiber: 5 gms

PREP TIME: **10-15 minutes**   COOK TIME: **8-10 hours**   Serves 4

2-2½ pounds beef pot roast or 2½ pounds beef-stew parts,
    preferably organic or all-natural

4 carrots, sliced

4 stalks celery, sliced

4 baking potatoes (Idaho or Russet), cut into 1-inch cubes

2 large onions, cut into ½-inch slices

3 cloves garlic, crushed

2 bay leaves

1 cup beef broth

Place the beef in a Crock-Pot. Top with the carrots, celery, potatoes, onions, garlic, bay leaves, and beef broth. Set the heat on low; cook for 8-10 hours or until fork-tender. Serve with natural au jus sauce.

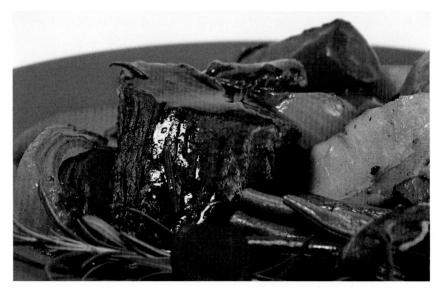

Teriyaki Steak

This is teriyaki steak at its best. The marinade is what makes it so mouthwateringly good. Take your time, and savor the flavor.

PREP TIME: **15-20 minutes (not counting marinating time)**

COOK TIME: **Approx. 6 minutes** · · · · · **Serves 4**

½ cup low-sodium soy sauce

½ cup honey

¼ cup red wine vinegar

3 teaspoons grated fresh ginger

2 cloves garlic, minced

½ cup canola oil

6 scallions, finely chopped

2 pounds skirt steak, thinly sliced, preferably organic or all-natural

In a large mixing bowl, combine all the ingredients except the steak; whisk thoroughly. Cut the steak on the bias into thin slices; add to the marinade and stir to coat. Cover and refrigerate from 30 minutes up to 24 hours. If cooking within 30 minutes, preheat oven on broil. For medium-cooked steak, broil one side only for 6 minutes.

NUTRITIONAL NOTE

For healthy people who don't need to avoid red meat, lean, organic beef eaten in moderation provides protein, B vitamins, zinc, iron, and selenium, a trace mineral essential for good health.

NUTRITION FACTS

(Per serving)

Calories: 209

Total Fat: 6 gms

Sodium: 16 mgs

Carbohydrates: 24 gms

Protein: 18 gms

Fiber: 2.2 gms

Sweet and Sour Sauce over Baby Back Ribs

You'll find many barbecue sauces in stores, but this homemade version truly hearkens back to the days of home-style cooking. It's so good you may never reach for store-bought again!

PREP TIME: **10 minutes**	COOK TIME: **35-40 minutes**	Serves 4

SAUCE

1 15-ounce bottle ketchup

1 cup light-brown sugar

2 tablespoons apple cider vinegar

1 teaspoon dry mustard

½ teaspoon garlic powder

¼ teaspoon black pepper

RIBS

2 racks baby back pork ribs, cut into individual ribs, preferably all-natural

TO MAKE SAUCE: Combine all sauce ingredients in a medium-size saucepan. Cook over low-medium heat for about 5 minutes, stirring constantly until thickened. Set the sauce aside.

TO COOK RIBS: Preheat the oven to 350°F. Bring a large sauce pot of water to a rolling boil over high heat. Lower the heat to medium and add the ribs. Cook for 10 minutes; drain. Arrange the ribs on 2 medium-size nonstick baking sheets. Bake for 10 minutes. Remove the ribs from the oven; drain. Brush the sauce liberally over the ribs. Bake for 10 more minutes. Serve immediately.

TIP: *Boiling the ribs helps remove some of the fat. But if you want to skip boiling them, arrange the ribs on 2 medium-size nonstick baking sheets and bake for 20 minutes. Remove the ribs from the oven; drain. Brush the sauce liberally over the ribs. Bake for 20 more minutes.*

NUTRITIONAL NOTE

Baby back ribs are cut from the loin, making them somewhat leaner and thinner than spareribs.

NUTRITION FACTS

(Per serving)

Calories: 290

Total Fat: 24 gms

Sodium: 230 mgs

Carbohydrates: 22 gms

Protein: 16 gms

Fiber: 0 gms

Lamb Shanks over Orzo Pasta

This family jewel had us all making a beeline for the dinner table when we were young. I guarantee that your family will declare this a favorite, as well. The lamb shanks take some time to cook but very little effort to prepare, and the result is meat so tender that it falls right off the bone.

PREP TIME: **15 minutes**   COOK TIME: **4-5 hours**   Serves 4

4 lamb shanks, preferably all-natural (look for smaller shanks to ensure they're not mutton)

1 tablespoons extra-virgin olive oil

1 whole yellow onion, diced

2 cloves garlic, crushed

2 28-ounce cans whole, peeled tomatoes, preferably Hunt's All-Natural, pureed*

2 15-ounce cans tomato sauce, preferably Hunt's All-Natural

½ teaspoon dried oregano

Small handful of fresh basil leaves, torn (or 1 teaspoon dried basil, crushed)

Black pepper to taste

¼ cup water, optional

Orzo pasta, whole wheat or enriched**

Fresh parsley, chopped (for garnish)

To puree tomatoes, put whole, peeled tomatoes into a blender or food processor and puree for 5 seconds, leaving tiny chunks of tomatoes for texture.

**Cook pasta according to package directions.*

In a large sauce pot over medium heat, brown shanks about 5-8 minutes on each side. Remove the shanks from the pot; set them aside. In the same pot, add 1 tablespoon of olive oil and the onion; sauté until the onion turns golden. Stir in the garlic and continue sautéing for another 2-3 minutes. Add the pureed tomatoes, tomato sauce, oregano, basil, and black pepper; stir thoroughly. Add the browned lamb shanks; stir again. Reduce the heat to simmer; partially cover. Cook for 4-5 hours, stirring occasionally. During cooking, skim any oil off the top with a spoon. Add the ¼ cup of water if the sauce gets too thick. When done, the meat will easily fall off bone. Serve piping hot over orzo. Sprinkle with chopped parsley.

Breaded Pork Chops Italiano

These pork chops cook up beautifully. They're moist, meaty, and rib-stickin' good!

Pork is a nutrient-dense food containing good amounts of vitamin B6, niacin, and thiamine, a key vitamin that helps with the metabolism of carbohydrates, protein, and fat.

NUTRITION FACTS

(Per serving)

Calories: 244

Total Fat: 11 gms

Sodium: 450 mgs

Carbohydrates: 14 gms

Protein: 23 gms

Fiber 2.2 gms

PREP TIME: **10 minutes**   COOK TIME: **35-40 minutes**   Serves 2-4

½ - ¾ cup Italian-style bread crumbs

2 teaspoons grated Parmesan cheese

1 teaspoon chopped fresh parsley

Salt and pepper to taste

1 egg

1 large clove garlic, minced

1 teaspoon water

4 bone-in pork chops, preferably all-natural, about 1-inch thick

½ cup low-sodium chicken broth

Preheat the oven to 350°F. On a large plate, combine the bread crumbs, cheese, parsley, salt, and pepper. Set it aside. In a small bowl, whisk together the egg, garlic, and water. One at a time, dredge each chop through the egg wash, and then through the bread-crumb mixture, thoroughly coating the entire chop. Place the chops in a 13 x 8½-inch baking dish and pour the broth over and around the chops. Bake uncovered for 35-40 minutes, or until the internal temperature reaches 155-160°F. with a meat thermometer. Serve immediately.

Spice 'Em Up Pork Chops

*Imagine melt-in-your-mouth pork chops exploding with spicy juices —
not spicy "hot," but spice that drips with flavor. These chops deliver with
a taste you won't forget!*

PREP TIME: **15 minutes (not counting marinating time)**

COOK TIME: **16 minutes**   Serves 2-4

MARINADE

2 cloves garlic, minced

6 scallions (green onions), finely chopped

1 tablespoon grated fresh ginger

2 teaspoons peppercorns, coarsely crushed

1 teaspoon cinnamon

½ teaspoon allspice

½ cup fresh apple cider

1 tablespoon low-sodium soy sauce

PORK CHOPS

2 tablespoons extra-virgin olive oil for sautéing

4 bone-in pork chops, preferably all-natural, about 1-inch thick

TO MARINATE CHOPS: In a large bowl, combine marinade ingredients and
rub over the pork chops, making sure to cover them evenly. Cover the
bowl and refrigerate from 1 hour up to 24 hours.

TO COOK CHOPS: Heat the olive oil in a large skillet over high heat for 1
minute. Reduce the heat to medium and add the marinated chops. Cook
for 8 minutes on the first side, 7 minutes on the second side. Remove the
chops from the heat and let stand for 5 minutes (to retain juices) before
serving.

NUTRITIONAL NOTE

Trim away the fat
from the pork chops,
and enjoy a meat
that's high in protein,
vitamin B_6, and niacin.

NUTRITION FACTS

(Per serving)

Calories: 319

Total Fat: 17.1 gms

Sodium: 162 mgs

Carbohydrates: 19.3 gms

Protein: 18.4 gms

Fiber: 1 gm

Mascarpone Stuffed Chicken with Marsala Date Sauce

The first time I made this dish for my family, my husband told me how much he enjoyed it so many times that I lost count. In a word, "Dee-licious!"

NUTRITIONAL NOTE

For a lower-fat version, substitute low-fat cream cheese for mascarpone cheese.

NUTRITION FACTS

(Per serving)

Calories: 498

Total Fat: 45.3 gms

Sodium: 451 mgs

Carbohydrates: 16.7 gms

Protein: 28.6 gms

Fiber: 5 gms

PREP TIME: **30 minutes**	COOK TIME: **Approx. 45 minutes**	Serves 4

4 boneless, skinless chicken breasts (about 2 pounds), preferably organic or all-natural

1 8-ounce container mascarpone cheese, softened

1 shallot, minced

2 tablespoons fresh chives, minced

¼ teaspoon balsamic vinegar

¼ cup grated Parmesan cheese

1 egg, slightly beaten

4 thin slices prosciutto, cut into small pieces

4 tablespoons extra-virgin olive oil, for searing

3 tablespoons finely chopped parsley for garnish

DATE SAUCE

3 tablespoons extra-virgin olive oil

1 yellow onion, cut into ¼-inch slices

2 cups marsala wine

8 medjool dates, quartered and pits removed

2 tablespoons honey

Zest of 1 orange

Black pepper to taste

TO MAKE STUFFING/TO STUFF CHICKEN: Rinse the chicken breasts under cold water; pat them dry. On a cutting board, using a paring knife, slice horizontally into the thickest side of each chicken breast to form a small pocket. Set the chicken aside. In a medium-size bowl, add the mascarpone, shallot, chives, vinegar, Parmesan, egg, and prosciutto. Stir thoroughly to combine. Fill each chicken-breast pocket generously, with at least 4 teaspoons of the cheese mixture.

TO MAKE DATE SAUCE: Heat 3 tablespoons of olive oil in a medium-size sauce pot over medium heat for 1-2 minutes. Add the onions and caramelize them, stirring often until the onions are a light golden color, about 10 minutes. Remove the pot from the heat. Add the marsala wine, dates, honey, and orange zest. Cook over medium heat for 10-15 minutes, stirring occasionally. Season with black pepper. Set the date sauce aside.

TO COOK CHICKEN: Preheat the oven to 425°F. Heat the 4 tablespoons of olive oil in a large, deep oven-safe skillet over high heat for 1 minute. Sear both sides of the chicken breasts, 2 minutes per side. Remove from the heat and pour the date sauce over chicken. Place the skillet in the oven and bake for 20 minutes, or until the internal temperature reaches 170°F. with a meat thermometer. Garnish with parsley, and serve immediately.

Curry Chicken

If you like curry but don't want too much heat in it, you'll love this recipe. I call it my "curry without worry." Even my brother raves over this dish, and that's saying a lot, considering he breaks into a cold sweat just looking at a chili pepper! I think you'll like the savory flavor and the nutty texture.

PREP TIME: **10 minutes**	COOK TIME: **25 minutes**	Serves 4

8 bone-in, skinless chicken thighs, preferably organic or all-natural

½ cup all-purpose flour, unbleached

¼ cup extra-virgin olive oil

1 yellow onion, sliced

2 tablespoons dried curry powder

Salt to taste

½ teaspoon black pepper

1 15-ounce can lentils, drained and rinsed

½ cup slivered almonds

2 cups low-sodium chicken broth

Rinse the chicken pieces under cold water; pat them dry. Spread the flour onto a medium-size plate. Dredge the chicken through the flour, covering each piece on both sides. Heat the olive oil in a large, deep skillet over high heat for 1 minute. Add the onion; sauté until golden brown, about 5 minutes, stirring occasionally. Place the floured chicken atop the cooked onions. Cook for 2 minutes on each side. Add the curry powder, salt, and pepper. Turn the chicken over again and stir in the lentils, almonds, and chicken broth. Cover and simmer for 8 minutes. Turn the chicken over again and simmer for 8 more minutes. If the liquid diminishes, add more broth.

Chicken in Light Beer Sauce

This dish comes straight from Naples, Italy. My friends Nadia and Marco once made it for my husband and me, and it was love at first bite! Every time I make this, the fragrant aroma fills our home, and before I know it, the family is in the kitchen asking, "When's dinner?" The tasty sauce tops off this "delish" dish.

PREP TIME: **20 minutes**   COOK TIME: **Approx. 55 minutes**   Serves 4

1 4-4½ pound whole chicken, cut-up, preferably organic or all-natural

½ cup all-purpose flour, unbleached

⅓ cup natural buttery spread (such as Earth Balance or Smart Balance)

1 medium to large yellow onion, chopped

3 slices cooked ham, cut into small pieces

1 clove garlic, minced

1 12-ounce bottle light beer

1 teaspoon chopped fresh parsley (or 1½ teaspoons dried parsley flakes)

¼ teaspoon black pepper

Rinse the chicken pieces under cold water; pat them dry. Spread the flour onto a large plate. Dredge the chicken pieces through the flour, covering each piece on both sides. Heat the butter alternative in an extra-large, deep skillet over medium heat. Add the floured chicken to the skillet; cook for 10 minutes on each side. Transfer the chicken to a plate; set it aside. In the same skillet, add the onion; sauté for 3 minutes, stirring occasionally. Add the ham, garlic, beer, parsley, and black pepper; stir thoroughly. Add the chicken back to the skillet and cover; cook for 30 minutes. ✿

NUTRITIONAL NOTE

Chicken provides protein, niacin, and vitamin B_6 for energy. Keeping the skin on when cooking adds to the overall flavor of the dish, but to trim your fat intake, remove skin after cooking.

NUTRITION FACTS

(Per serving)

Calories: 469

Total Fat: 11.5 gms

Sodium: 97.5 mgs

Carbohydrates: 26 gms

Protein: 46 gms

Fiber: 3 gms

Roasted Lemon-Pepper Chicken

This meal takes just a few minutes to prepare. So, pop it in the oven, put up your feet, and relax for 90 minutes while it cooks. When the timer goes off, your meal is ready to eat.

PREP TIME: **15 minutes**	COOK TIME: **90 minutes**	Serves 4

1 4-pound whole chicken, preferably organic or all-natural

3 whole cloves garlic

1 lemon, cut in half

1 tablespoon lemon pepper

6-8 small red roasting potatoes, quartered

1 tablespoon extra-virgin olive oil

1 teaspoon fresh rosemary (or 1½ teaspoons dried rosemary)

Pinch of salt

3 medium carrots, cut into ½-inch slices

1 large yellow onion, chopped

½ cup low-sodium chicken broth

NUTRITIONAL NOTE
Your eyes will thank you for the beta-carotene you get by eating carrots. Potatoes are free of fat and cholesterol and are high in potassium.

NUTRITION FACTS
(Per serving)
Calories: 250
Total Fat: 9 gms
Sodium: 400 mgs
Carbohydrates: 35 gms
Protein: 15 gms
Fiber: 5 gms

Preheat the oven to 375°F. Rinse the chicken under cold water; pat it dry. Place the garlic cloves in the chicken cavity along with one lemon half. Place the chicken in a 15 x 10-inch baking dish. Squeeze the second lemon half over the bird. Sprinkle lemon pepper over the chicken and rub it in. In a medium-size bowl, add the potatoes and olive oil; sprinkle with the rosemary and salt. Using your hands, toss lightly to coat. Arrange the potatoes, carrots, and onion around the exterior of the chicken in the baking dish. Pour the chicken broth over the vegetables. Bake for 90 minutes. Baste after 45 minutes, and a few times during cooking.

Turkey and Blue Cheese Burgers

I'm a burger lover from way back, not only because they taste sensational, but because you can create any kind of burger your little heart desires. Make this version, and you'll never have to ask, "Where's the beef?"

NUTRITIONAL NOTE

Dark turkey meat actually contains higher amounts of zinc, riboflavin, and thiamin than white turkey meat. White turkey meat has about 20 fewer calories than dark meat.

NUTRITION FACTS

(Per serving)
Calories: 260
Total Fat: 18 gms
Sodium: 457 mgs
Carbohydrates: 11 gms
Protein: 28 gms
Fiber: 3 gms

PREP TIME: **20 minutes**   COOK TIME: **Approx. 25 minutes**   Serves 6

SAUCE

¼ cup ketchup

¼ cup light mayonnaise

Pinch of black pepper

Salt to taste

BURGERS

1 ½ pounds dark meat ground turkey, preferably organic or all-natural

1 teaspoon Worcestershire sauce

½ teaspoon black pepper

½ teaspoon garlic powder

¼ cup green onions, diced

2 heaping tablespoons crumbled blue cheese

4 tablespoons extra-virgin olive oil

1 yellow onion, sliced

12 ounces sliced mushrooms

Pinch of salt and pepper

6 whole-wheat buns

TO MAKE SAUCE: In a small bowl, add all the sauce ingredients and whisk until thoroughly combined. Set the sauce aside.

TO MAKE BURGERS: In a large bowl, combine the ground turkey, Worcestershire sauce, pepper, garlic powder, diced scallions and blue cheese. Mix thoroughly with your hands and form into 4-inch patties; set them aside.

Heat 2 tablespoons of olive oil in a large skillet over medium-high heat for 1-2 minutes. Add the sliced onion, mushrooms and a pinch of salt and pepper; sauté for 12-15 minutes, until onions are golden, stirring occasionally. Cover to keep it warm; set aside. Heat the remaining 2 tablespoons of olive oil in a large skillet over medium heat for 2 minutes. Add the burgers and cook for about 5½ minutes on each side.

Place some sauce and a burger onto a warm whole-wheat bun. Top with sautéed onions and mushrooms. Serve immediately.

Chicken Cutlets with Mushrooms and Mozzarella

These chicken cutlets are habit-forming. It will be nearly impossible to put down your fork.

NUTRITIONAL NOTE

Chicken is the world's primary source of protein. It's also a good source of selenium, a trace mineral essential to good health, and vitamin B_6.

NUTRITION FACTS

(Per serving)
Calories: 215
Total Fat: 18 gms
Sodium: 200 mgs
Carbohydrates: 25 gms
Protein: 34 gms
Fiber: 1.4 gms

PREP TIME: **20 minutes**   COOK TIME: **30-35 minutes**   Serves 4

CHICKEN CUTLETS

2-2½ pounds chicken cutlets, preferably organic or all-natural

3-4 eggs

1½ teaspoons cold water

2-2½ cups Italian-style bread crumbs

2 tablespoons chopped fresh parsley

¼ cup extra-virgin olive oil, plus 3-4 tablespoons for each new batch

MUSHROOM AND MOZZARELLA TOPPING

2 cups chopped fresh mushrooms

2 tablespoons extra-virgin olive oil

Salt and pepper to taste

Part-skim mozzarella cheese, thinly sliced, 1-2 slices per cutlet

TO PREPARE CUTLETS: Rinse the chicken cutlets under cold water; pat them dry. Place each cutlet inside a piece of plastic wrap. Gently pound them with a meat tenderizer until each cutlet is very thin; set them aside. Beat the eggs and water in a medium-size bowl. Spread the bread crumbs out onto a large plate, add the parsley, and combine. Dredge each cutlet through the egg wash, then through the bread crumbs. Place the coated cutlets on a clean plate and refrigerate for 30 minutes.

TO PREPARE TOPPING: Using a damp paper towel, gently clean the mushrooms. On a cutting board, slice or chop them into bite-size pieces. Heat 2 tablespoons of olive oil in a medium size skillet over medium heat for 1-2 minutes. Stir in the mushrooms, salt, and pepper; sauté until soft. Set aside and cover to keep warm. After 30 minutes, preheat the oven to 375° F.

TO COOK CUTLETS: In an extra-large skillet, add the ¼ cup of olive oil, heat for 1-2 minutes. Add some of the cutlets; cook until golden, about 2 minutes on each side. Transfer the cutlets onto a plate lined with a paper towel to absorb any excess oil; cover to keep them warm. Cook the rest of the cutlets in batches, adding 3-4 tablespoons of olive oil to the skillet for each new batch.

TO ASSEMBLE: Place the cutlets on 2-3 large, nonstick baking sheets. Arrange the cooked mushrooms on top of each cutlet; top each with 1-2 slices of mozzarella. Bake until the cheese is melted, about 5 minutes.

Turkey Chili

For a chili with a bit more protein, try this recipe. The turkey adds texture and makes for a hearty and healthful meal. So gobble up and enjoy!

NUTRITIONAL NOTE
Turkey provides protein and contains only about half the amount of saturated fat found in regular red meat.

NUTRITION FACTS
(Per serving)
Calories: 370
Total Fat: 17.4 gms
Sodium: 296 mgs
Carbohydrates: 37 gms
Protein: 25 gms
Fiber: 4 gms

PREP TIME: 15 minutes   **COOK TIME:** Approx. 45 minutes   Serves 4

TURKEY AND VEGETABLES MIXTURE

2 tablespoons extra-virgin olive oil

1 pound ground turkey breast or thighs, preferably organic or all-natural

1 cup diced yellow onion

1 cup diced celery

1 cup sliced carrots

2 cloves garlic, crushed

BEANS AND TOMATOES MIXTURE

1 15-ounce can red kidney beans, drained and rinsed well

1 15-ounce can diced tomatoes, drained

1 8-ounce can tomato sauce

1-2 cups low-sodium chicken broth, start with 1 cup and add more during cooking if needed

½ teaspoon crushed red chili peppers, or chili powder

1 tablespoon paprika

1 teaspoon salt

½ teaspoon cracked black pepper

Heat the olive oil in a large sauce pot over medium heat for 1 minute. Add the turkey and cook for 3 minutes, or until browned. Stir to break up any large pieces. Add the onion, celery, carrots, and garlic. Continue cooking for 5 minutes over medium heat, stirring occasionally. While the turkey is cooking, in a large mixing bowl, combine all of the ingredients for the beans and tomatoes mixture. Reduce the heat under the sauce pot and add the beans and tomatoes mixture. Stir thoroughly, partially cover, and cook for 30 minutes over low-medium heat, stirring occasionally. Add more chicken broth if needed. Taste-test the chili while it's cooking; adjust seasoning as needed. Serve the chili in warm bowls along with whole-grain or whole-wheat garlic bread. Corn bread is good, too!

Chicken Cacciatore

This delectable chicken cacciatore is an authentic Italian treasure. It's easy to prepare and different from the usual recipe in that it contains no mushrooms, onions, peppers, or tomatoes. You'll love what the olives and anchovy paste do for this dish—mmm good! Try it with my side dish of Artichoke Hearts with Potatoes (see page 97).

PREP TIME: **10 minutes**   COOK TIME: **Approx. 40 minutes**   Serves 4

1 4-4½ pound whole chicken, preferably organic, cut up

¼ cup extra-virgin olive oil

1 tablespoon dried rosemary

2 cloves garlic, peeled

¼ teaspoon black pepper

1 chicken bouillon cube, crushed

¾ cup red wine vinegar

1 tube Italian anchovy paste

1 12-ounce jar pitted kalamata olives, with liquid

Salt to taste

Rinse the chicken pieces under cold water; pat them dry. Heat the olive oil in an extra-large, deep skillet over medium heat for 1-2 minutes. Add the chicken pieces, rosemary, garlic, and black pepper; partially cover. Cook for 20 minutes, turning occasionally. Add the bouillon, vinegar, and anchovy paste; stir thoroughly. Reduce the heat. Add the olives; partially cover. Cook for 20 more minutes, stirring and turning occasionally. Add salt to taste. (You may have to cook the breasts for 2 minutes longer than the rest of the chicken.)

Vegetables and Side Dishes

Garlic Rapini

Wilted Spinach

Creamy Baked Cauliflower

Italian Style Stuffed Artichokes

Stuffed Peppers a la Zappala

Cheesy Asparagus

Artichoke Hearts with Potatoes

Zucchini Casserole

Mom's Rice and Sausage Special

Oven-Roasted Brussels Sprouts and Garlic
with Crispy Bacon

Baked Sweet Potato Fries

Toasted Pecan and Scallion Brown Rice

Maple Pecan Glazed Carrots

Steamed Broccoli with Hollandaise Sauce

Garlic Rapini

Rapini, also known as broccoli rabe, is a vegetable that resembles thin broccoli stalks. It has leaves similar to turnip greens. This Italian favorite has a bold taste and offers a treasure trove of nutrients. Acquire a taste for this exceptional vegetable, and your health will thank you for it.

NUTRITIONAL NOTE

Rapini is a very good source of fiber, protein, vitamins A and C, calcium, and iron.

NUTRITION FACTS

(Per serving)

Calories: 70

Total Fat: 5 gms

Sodium: 66 mgs

Carbohydrates: 3 gms

Protein: 2 gms

Fiber: 2 gms

PREP TIME: **5 minutes**   COOK TIME: **Approx. 20 minutes**   Serves 4

1 bunch rapini (about 1¼ pounds)*

2 cups water

2 large cloves garlic, whole

½ teaspoon salt

¼ cup extra-virgin olive oil

¼ teaspoon crushed red pepper or ¼ teaspoon black pepper

*The small yellow flowers you sometimes see blooming amid the rapini greens are edible.

Rinse the rapini under cold water; pat it dry. Trim away and discard bottom half of stems, about 1 inch. In a large, deep skillet over medium heat, add the water, garlic, and salt; bring to a boil. Add the rapini; cook for 5 minutes. Stir and cover. Cook for another 7-10 minutes until the rapini is tender and bright green. Add the olive oil and pepper of your choice. Stir and serve.

Wilted Spinach

This nutritious dish takes no more than 5 minutes to prepare — from the skillet to your dinner plate. You'll appreciate its delicate taste. Serve it with my Baked Salmon (see page 54) for a quick and healthful meal.

PREP TIME: **5 minutes**	COOK TIME: **3-5 minutes**	Serves 4

2 tablespoons extra-virgin olive oil

2 cloves garlic, crushed

1 large bunch fresh large-leaf spinach or 15 ounces fresh baby spinach,
    rinsed well and dried

Pinch of salt

Crushed red pepper or black pepper to taste

Heat the olive oil in an extra-large, deep skillet over medium heat for 1 minute. Stir in the garlic and spinach; toss until the spinach is wilted. Add the salt and pepper of your choice to taste. Stir and serve.

NUTRITIONAL NOTE

Spinach is a good source of iron, as well as vitamins A and C. It's also considered a negative-calorie food and one of the most nutrient-dense foods available.

NUTRITION FACTS

(Per serving)
Calories: 69
Total Fat: 5 gms
Sodium: 72 mgs
Carbohydrates: 4 gms
Protein: 2.2 gms
Fiber: 1 gm

Creamy Baked Cauliflower

This dish is rich and downright delectable. The kids will love it for its creamy, cheesy taste and so will you!

PREP TIME: **10 minutes**   COOK TIME: **Approx. 40 minutes**   Serves 4

---

1 head fresh cauliflower, or 16 ounces frozen cauliflower florets (in bag)

1 cup water

2½ tablespoons natural buttery spread (such as Earth Balance or
    Smart Balance)

2 heaping tablespoons flour

½ teaspoon nutmeg

¼ teaspoon black pepper

1 cup heavy cream or 1 cup 1% low-fat milk for a lower-fat version

1 tablespoon shredded sharp Cheddar cheese or your
    favorite low-fat cheese

1 tablespoon grated Parmesan cheese

Salt to taste

Preheat the oven to 390°F. Rinse the fresh cauliflower under cold water; pat it dry. Remove the leaves and the stem. Cut the cauliflower into florets, slicing larger florets in half and trimming away any brown spots. In a medium size saucepot, over medium-high heat, add 1 cup of water and the florets, cover and bring to a boil, about 7-8 minutes. Reduce heat and let cook until they're tender-crisp but not soft, about 5 minutes. If using frozen cauliflower, follow the package cooking directions, removing from heat when tender-crisp.

Drain cauliflower and arrange in an 11 x 7-inch baking dish or a 1½ -quart casserole dish. Set it aside. In a medium-size sauce pot, over medium heat, melt the butter alternative. Stir in the flour, nutmeg, and black pepper. Gradually add the cream or low-fat milk, stirring until the mixture combines and thickens, about 2 minutes. Pour the sauce over the cauliflower in the baking dish; stir to coat. Sprinkle the Cheddar and Parmesan cheeses on top. Bake for 20 minutes. Serve immediately.

NUTRITIONAL NOTE

Cauliflower is a good source of protein, niacin, and fiber. If you're watching calories, using the low-fat milk instead of the cream works well.

NUTRITION FACTS

(Using heavy cream)
(Per serving)
Calories: 348
Total Fat: 30.5 gms
Sodium: 179 mgs
Carbohydrates: 15.5 gms
Protein: 6 gms
Fiber: 3.75 gms

(Using low-fat milk)
Calories: 170
Total Fat: 9 gms
Sodium: 182 mgs
Carbohydrates: 17 gms
Protein: 7 gms
Fiber: 3.75 gms

Italian-Style Stuffed Artichokes

These stuffed artichokes are a big hit in our home. When the green, globe-size artichokes, noted for their big hearts, are on sale, buy a couple extra. Your family will love you for it, and you'll know you're providing a dish that's delicious and nutritious.

NUTRITIONAL NOTE

Artichokes, especially good in late spring, summer, and fall, are packed with fiber, potassium, iron, and calcium, as well as other trace elements essential for good health.

NUTRITION FACTS

(Per serving)

Calories: 140
Total Fat: 5.95 gms
Sodium: 320 mgs
Carbohydrates: 24.4 gms
Protein: 8.4 gms
Fiber: 6 gms

PREP TIME: **20 minutes**   COOK TIME: **1 hour, 20 minutes**   Serves 4

4 globe artichokes

1 cup Italian-style bread crumbs

1 tablespoon fresh parsley, chopped

2 cloves garlic, minced

1 cup grated Parmesan cheese

1 teaspoon each: salt and black pepper

4 tablespoons extra-virgin olive oil

2 cups water for steaming, or 4 cups if using two pots

On a cutting board, using a serrated edged knife, cut ¼-½ inch off the tops of the artichokes. On the bottom portion, cut off the stems so the artichokes sit flat. Rinse the artichokes in cold water; turn them upside down to drain. In a large bowl, thoroughly mix together the bread crumbs, parsley, garlic, Parmesan cheese, salt, and pepper. Starting from the bottom of the artichoke and working up, open the leaves and sprinkle with some of the bread-crumb mixture. Continue until each artichoke is packed all the way to the top. Drizzle 1 tablespoon of olive oil over the top and around the sides of each artichoke.

Heat 2 cups of water in a large sauce pot over low heat. Place the artichokes bottom side down in the pot. (Depending on the artichokes' size, two pots may be needed.) Cover and steam about 1 hour, 20 minutes over low heat. Check every 30 minutes to make sure the water does not evaporate; add more water as needed. The artichokes are done when their leaves are tender and pull away with little effort. (To avoid burns, use tongs to gently pull out the leaves to test doneness.)

TIP: *While I love artichoke leaves, I think the heart is the best part. So, when you're eating them and get down to the bottom where the very small, very soft leaves are, slice the leaves off along with the fuzzy middles. Sprinkle a pinch of salt on it and bite into one of nature's best-tasting treats!*

Stuffed Peppers
à la Zappala

Mom made these peppers once a week because she knew how much we all loved them. She used green peppers, which work just fine, but red peppers are a little sweeter, and I love how they pop with color. Select your favorite.

NUTRITIONAL NOTE
Although bell peppers contain many nutrients, especially vitamin C, they're also one of the most heavily sprayed vegetables, so make sure to thoroughly rinse them. When you can, try buying organic bell peppers.

NUTRITION FACTS
(Per serving)
Calories: 321
Total Fat: 22 gms
Sodium: 72 mgs
Carbohydrates: 15 gms
Protein: 39 gms
Fiber: 5 gms

PREP TIME: **30 minutes**   COOK TIME: **Approx. 50 minutes**   Serves 4

4 bell peppers, preferably organic

1 pound beef, pork, and veal (3-in-1 pack), preferably organic
    or all-natural

1 tablespoon extra-virgin olive oil

1 yellow onion, diced

2 cloves garlic, minced

1 15-ounce can diced tomatoes

½ teaspoon dried oregano

½ teaspoon dried basil

1 tablespoon freshly grated Parmesan or Locatelli cheese

½ teaspoon each: salt and pepper

¼ cup shredded part-skim mozzarella cheese for topping

Preheat the oven to 350°F. Bring a large sauce pot of water to a boil. Meanwhile, cut the tops off the peppers and discard. Rinse the peppers under cold water; pat them dry. Remove the seeds and membranes. When the water comes to a boil, reduce the heat to medium, and add the peppers, making sure they're submerged; cook for 10 minutes, turning occasionally until the peppers are tender but not too soft. While the peppers are cooking, in a large skillet over medium heat, cook the meat until it's browned, about 6-7 minutes, breaking it up into small pieces. Drain off the fat, and set pan aside. When the peppers are tender, remove them from the pot and run them under cold water to cool; pat them dry. Arrange the peppers cut-side up in a baking dish; set them aside.

Heat 1 tablespoon of olive oil in a medium-size skillet for 1 minute. Add the onion; sauté until translucent, about 4-5 minutes. Add the garlic; cook for 2 more minutes. Return the skillet with the cooked meat to the stove over medium heat. Add the diced tomatoes and the cooked onion and garlic; stir to combine. Add the oregano, basil, Parmesan or Locatelli cheese, salt, and pepper; mix thoroughly. Remove from the heat. Fill each pepper to the top with the meat mixture. Bake for 30 minutes. Remove from the oven, top with mozzarella cheese. Bake for 5 more minutes. Serve hot.

Cheesy Asparagus

This versatile recipe takes little time to prepare and will complement almost any entrée. I make these with my Fish Under Wraps (see page 61), and dinner is on the table in 20 minutes.

NUTRITIONAL NOTE

Asparagus is a good source of calcium and iodine, and an excellent source of folic acid.

NUTRITION FACTS

(Per serving)
Calories: 150
Total Fat: 7 gms
Sodium: 320 mgs
Carbohydrates: 4 gms
Protein: 7 gms
Fiber: 2 gms

PREP TIME: **5 minutes**	COOK TIME: **14 minutes**	Serves 4

1 bunch fresh asparagus (about 1 pound)*

1 tablespoon extra-virgin olive oil

½ teaspoon black pepper

4 slices Taleggio cheese

*Slightly thicker asparagus works best for this recipe.

Preheat the oven to 390°F. Rinse the asparagus under cold water, pat dry, and break off the ends. (Bend them and they'll snap off naturally.) In a medium-size bowl, add the asparagus, olive oil, and black pepper. Using your hands, toss lightly to coat. On a large, nonstick baking sheet, arrange the asparagus in a single layer. Bake for 12 minutes. Remove the asparagus from the oven and layer cheese slices over them. Return the asparagus to the oven for 2 minutes. Serve hot.

TIP: *Taleggio cheese has a strong smell, but the taste is smooth and mild, and it melts nicely over the asparagus. If you prefer, you can use my Hollandaise Sauce (see page 106) in place of the cheese.*

Artichoke Hearts with Potatoes

The taste and texture of this dish is home-style cooking just the way Mom used to make. Pair it with my Chicken Cacciatore (see page 84) or another poultry dish for a delicious meal.

PREP TIME: **10 minutes**	COOK TIME: **25-30 minutes**	Serves 4

3 tablespoons extra-virgin olive oil

2 whole cloves garlic

3-4 medium white potatoes, peeled and cut into bite-size chunks

1 9-ounce package frozen artichoke hearts, cut into square chunks

1 tablespoon chopped fresh parsley (or ½ teaspoon dried parsley flakes)

1 teaspoon salt

½ teaspoon black pepper

Heat 2 tablespoons of olive oil in a medium-size sauce pot over medium heat for 1 minute. Add the garlic and potatoes; stir. Partially cover and cook for 15 minutes, stirring occasionally. Add the artichoke hearts, parsley, the remaining 1 tablespoon of olive oil, salt, and pepper. Cook for 10-15 minutes more or until the potatoes are fork-tender.

NUTRITIONAL NOTE

Artichoke hearts are full of nutrients including potassium, folic acid, and magnesium.

NUTRITION FACTS

(Per serving)

Calories: 193

Total Fat: 12 gms

Sodium: 200 mgs

Carbohydrates: 21.5 gms

Protein: 5.6 gms

Fiber: 4 gms

Zucchini Casserole

Casseroles have been a long-standing comfort food, and this one is no exception. The ingredients make for a side dish that's packed with great taste and critical nutrients. Hope you're hungry!

PREP TIME: **20-25 minutes**

COOK TIME: **Approx. 35-40 minutes   Serves 4-5**

4 fresh medium zucchini with smooth, unblemished skins,
    preferably organic

1 cup low-sodium vegetable broth

2 eggs

15 whole-grain crackers, for grinding

1 tablespoon extra-virgin olive oil

1 large yellow onion, diced

2 cloves garlic, minced

½ cup natural buttery spread (such as Earth Balance or
    Smart Balance), softened

¼ teaspoon salt

½ teaspoon black pepper

Preheat the oven to 350°F. Rinse the zucchini under cold water; pat dry. Cut the zucchini into small chunks. In a large sauce pot over medium heat, add the zucchini and broth. Cook until soft, about 15-20 minutes. As the zucchini is cooking, beat the eggs lightly in a small bowl; set them aside. In a food processor, grind the crackers; set them aside. Heat the olive oil in a medium-size skillet over medium heat for 2 minutes. Add the onion and garlic; sauté for 5-7 minutes until golden.

When the zucchini is tender, drain it in a colander, making sure to remove all liquid. Return the zucchini to the pot. Add the butter alternative, salt, and pepper; mash together. Add the cooked onion-and-garlic mixture, eggs, and ¼ cup of the cracker crumbs; combine thoroughly. Transfer the vegetable mixture to a 2-quart casserole dish. Sprinkle the top with the remaining ¼ cup of cracker crumbs. Bake for 15-20 minutes until bubbling. Serve immediately.

Mom's Rice and Sausage Special

We had this easy-to-prepare, savory rice-and-sausage combination nearly every Thanksgiving, but it's delicious any time of year.

PREP TIME: **20-25 minutes**   COOK TIME: **45 minutes**   Serves 4-5

1 cup brown rice, uncooked

2-2½ cups low-sodium chicken broth

1 tablespoon extra-virgin olive oil

1 tablespoon natural buttery spread (such as Earth Balance or Smart Balance)

1 large yellow onion, finely diced

1 cup carrots, finely diced

1 cup celery, finely diced

1 pound mild Italian-style all-natural turkey sausage, casings removed

1 teaspoon dried Italian seasoning, crushed

¼ cup fresh chopped parsley (or 1 teaspoon dried parsley flakes)

Salt and cracked black pepper to taste

Cook the rice according to package directions, subsituting chicken broth for water. While the rice is cooking, heat the olive oil and butter alternative in a large skillet over medium heat for 1-2 minutes. Add the onion, carrots, and celery; sauté for 15 minutes, stirring occasionally. When rice is done, pour it into a large serving dish; cover it to keep it warm. Add the cooked onion mixture to the cooked rice in the serving dish; cover. In the same skillet, add the sausage; cook for about 10 minutes until browned, stirring to break up any large pieces. Add the Italian seasoning, parsley, salt, and pepper to the sausage; stir well. Combine the cooked sausage with the rice-and-vegetable mixture. Serve immediately.

Oven-Roasted Brussels Sprouts and Garlic with Crispy Bacon

My son, who's not so keen on brussels sprouts, will actually eat these. He says he likes the brussels sprouts with the crispy bacon and melted cheese on top. I say, "Hallelujah!"

PREP TIME: **15 minutes**   COOK TIME: **35 minutes**   Serves 4

1-1¼ pounds fresh brussels sprouts

6 slices center-cut bacon, preferably uncured*

6 cloves garlic, sliced lengthwise

2 tablespoons extra-virgin olive oil

Salt and pepper to taste

¼ cup grated sharp Italian cheese (Locatelli or Reggiano)

Uncured bacon is all natural, with no additives, nitrates, or artificial ingredients.

Preheat the oven to 375°F. Rinse brussels sprouts under cold water; pat them dry. On a cutting board, cut off and discard the bottom of each brussels sprout, then cut the sprout lengthwise. Cook the bacon until browned in a large skillet over medium heat. Cut the cooked bacon into small pieces. In a medium-size bowl, add the cooked bacon, brussels sprouts, garlic cloves, and olive oil. Season the mixture lightly with salt and pepper to taste. Using your hands, toss lightly to coat. Arrange the mixture on a medium-size, nonstick baking sheet. Roast for 25 minutes or until the sprouts are fork-tender. Add the cheese during the final few minutes; let the cheese melt. Serve immediately.

NUTRITIONAL NOTE

The large amount of vitamin A in brussels sprouts helps the body fight infection and promotes healthy, glowing skin.

NUTRITION FACTS

(Per serving)

Calories: 120

Total Fat: 9 gms

Sodium: 242 mgs

Carbohydrates: 7 gms

Protein: 7 gms

Fiber: 3 gms

Baked Sweet-Potato Fries

These "fries" may just convince you that your favorite spuds don't have to be deep-fried to taste great.

PREP TIME: **10 minutes**   COOK TIME: **50 minutes**   Serves 4

2 medium sweet potatoes, uniform in size

Salt to taste

¼ teaspoon cracked black pepper

1 tablespoon extra-virgin olive oil, plus a little extra for the baking sheets

Preheat the oven to 350°F. Fill a medium-size sauce pot with water, place over high heat, cover, and bring to a boil. While the water is heating, scrub the potatoes under cold water with a vegetable brush; dry them with a paper towel. (Keep the skin on for added taste and nutrients). Lightly oil 2 large, nonstick baking sheets, and set aside. When the water comes to a boil, reduce the heat to medium and add the potatoes; cook for 15 minutes. Remove the potatoes from the water and let them cool for a few minutes.

On a cutting board, cut off and discard the ends of the potatoes. Cut each potato in half lengthwise. Place flat side down and cut ¼-inch slices lengthwise. In a medium-size bowl, add the potatoes, salt to taste, black pepper, and 1 tablespoon of olive oil. Using your hands, toss lightly to coat. Arrange the potatoes in a single layer on prepared baking sheets. Bake for 35 minutes. Rotate the pan so the potatoes cook evenly. For slightly crispy potatoes, turn the oven temperature to broil, and cook 2-3 more minutes. Serve immediately. ✤

TIP: *Precooking the potatoes for 15 minutes makes them just soft enough to slice easily.*

NUTRITIONAL NOTE

You can use either sweet potatoes or yams. They are two different vegetables, but both work fine for this recipe. Both are nutrient rich and contain a lot of beta-carotene and fiber, but sweet potatoes contain more vitamins A and C than yams.

NUTRITION FACTS

(Per serving)

Calories: 102

Total Fat: 4 gms

Sodium: 41 mgs

Carbohydrates: 17 gms

Protein: 1 gm

Fiber: 3 gms

Toasted Pecan
and Scallion Brown Rice

This recipe kicks brown rice up a few notches. You may never eat plain brown rice again.

NUTRITIONAL NOTE

Aside from adding a delicious, crunchy texture to this dish, pecans offer a good source of protein and fiber, and contain no cholesterol.

PREP TIME: **10 minutes**	COOK TIME: **Approx. 40 minutes**	Serves 4

1 cup brown rice, uncooked

2-2½ cups low-sodium chicken broth

2 tablespoons natural buttery spread (such as Earth Balance
    or Smart Balance), or extra-virgin olive oil

1 shallot, diced

4 scallions (green onions), finely chopped

Salt and pepper to taste

¼ cup coarsely chopped pecans, toasted*

1 clove garlic, finely chopped

NUTRITION FACTS

(Per serving)
Calories: 420
Total Fat: 26.5 gms
Sodium: 46 mgs
Carbohydrates: 37.9 gms
Protein: 6.8 gms
Fiber: 4 gms

*To toast the pecans, place them on baking sheet and bake about 5 minutes at 350°F. Remove from the oven; set them aside. Turn off oven.

In a medium-size sauce pot, cook the rice according to package directions, substituting chicken broth for water. When done, set the cooked rice aside. While the rice is cooking, heat the butter alternative or olive oil in a large skillet over medium heat for 1-2 minutes. Add shallot and scallions. Sauté for 3 minutes. Add garlic and cook 1-2 minutes more; remove from the heat. Add the toasted pecans, cooked rice, salt, and pepper to the skillet. Stir thoroughly to combine. Serve hot.

Maple Pecan Glazed Carrots

Many parents find it difficult to get their children to eat carrots, but this recipe will make the job a cinch. Once the kids taste the sweetness of the maple syrup and the toasty, tasty pecans, they'll forget they're eating a vegetable. This is more like a sweet treat, one the whole family will enjoy.

PREP TIME: **10 minutes**   COOK TIME: **Approx. 20 minutes**   Serves 4

---

3 cups water

Pinch of salt

1 pound carrots, peeled and sliced in rounds

2 tablespoons extra-virgin olive oil

½ Vidalia onion, roughly chopped

½ cup pecans, chopped

¼ cup pure organic Vermont maple syrup

Salt and black pepper to taste

Bring the water and a pinch of salt to a boil in a medium-size sauce pot over high heat. Reduce the heat to medium and add the carrots. Boil for about 8 minutes or until fork-tender. Drain the carrots; set them aside. Heat the olive oil in a large skillet over medium heat for 1-2 minutes. Add the chopped onion; sauté until golden, about 6 minutes.

Add the cooked carrots and the pecans to the onion in the skillet; cook for 2-3 minutes until the pecans begin to toast. Add the maple syrup to the skillet; mix into the rest of the ingredients. Cook for 30 seconds more or until the mixture just begins to boil. Add salt and pepper to taste. Serve immediately.

NUTRITIONAL NOTE

Carrots are an excellent source of beta-carotene, which our bodies process into vitamin A, necessary for healthy skin and good night vision.

NUTRITION FACTS

(Per serving)

Calories: 359

Total Fat: 27 gms

Sodium: 19 mgs

Carbohydrates: 35 gms

Protein: 10 gms

Fiber: 4 gms

Steamed Broccoli with Hollandaise Sauce

Mom would whip up this delightful dish to make us kids eat our broccoli, and it worked! This updated version of an old recipe is lighter, and lower in fat. Even the pickiest eaters will enjoy what this sauce does for broccoli.

NUTRITIONAL NOTE

Steaming your broccoli is a healthful way to eat this all-important cruciferous vegetable. By doing so, you're getting nearly as many vitamins, minerals, and antioxidants as you would by eating it raw.

NUTRITION FACTS

(Per serving)
Calories: 200
Total Fat: 16 gms
Sodium: 38 mgs
Carbohydrates: 5.6 gms
Protein: 13 gms
Fiber: 2 gms

PREP TIME: **10 minutes**   COOK TIME: **Approx. 10 minutes**   Serves 4-5

BROCCOLI

1 large bunch fresh broccoli, or 1 16-ounce bag frozen broccoli florets

2 cups water

1 clove garlic, crushed

Salt and pepper to taste

HOLLANDAISE SAUCE

½ cup natural buttery spread (such as Earth Balance or Smart Balance)

3 egg yolks

2 tablespoons lemon juice

Dash of salt

Dash of cayenne pepper

TO PREPARE BROCCOLI: Rinse the broccoli under cold water; pat it dry. Cut it into bite-size pieces. Bring the water to a boil in a medium-size sauce pot over high heat. Reduce the heat. Place a steamer basket in the pot; add the broccoli and garlic to the basket. Cover and steam for 6-8 minutes or until the broccoli turns bright green and is fork-tender.

TO MAKE HOLLANDAISE SAUCE: While the broccoli is cooking, melt the butter alternative in a small saucepan over low heat. In a blender, combine the egg yolks, lemon juice, salt, and a dash cayenne pepper; cover and quickly pulse until blended. Slowly add the melted butter alternative; cover and blend.

TO ASSEMBLE: Place the cooked broccoli in a serving dish. Add salt and pepper to taste. Drizzle the hollandaise sauce over the broccoli. Serve immediately.

Desserts

Save-the-Day Sour Cream Coffee Cake

Pumpkin Cheesecake

Chocolate Torte

Frosted Walnut Brownies

Tiramisu

Key Lime Pie

Crescent Cookies

Mondel Bread

Dad's Favorite Pignoli Cookies

Mandarin Orange-Walnut and Sour Cream Jello

Baked Apples

Save-the-Day
Sour Cream Coffee Cake

The story goes that whenever Mom and Dad had a disagreement and Mom knew she was wrong, she would make Dad's favorite cake instead of apologizing, and all was forgiven. It must have worked…they were happily married for 50 years! I have updated the recipe to make it more healthful, but it's just as tasty. Enjoy it! (We still haven't gotten an answer from Dad as to what he would do when he was wrong.)

NUTRITIONAL NOTE
The two butter alternatives I suggest using contain no trans fats and work equally well for both baking and cooking.

NUTRITION FACTS
(Per serving)
Calories: 571
Total Fat: 26 gms
Sodium: 81 mgs
Carbohydrates: 87.2 gms
Protein: 22 gms
Fiber: 4 gms

PREP TIME: **15 minutes**	COOK TIME: **45 minutes**	Serves 8-10

CRUMB MIXTURE

1 cup chopped pecans or walnuts

¼ cup organic cane sugar or soft dark-brown sugar

1½ teaspoons cinnamon

½ teaspoon unprocessed cocoa

CAKE

½ cup natural buttery spread (such as Earth Balance or
    Smart Balance), softened

1¼ cups soft dark-brown sugar, packed

2 eggs

1 cup sour cream

1 teaspoon vanilla

2 cups whole-wheat pastry flour, sifted

1½ teaspoon baking powder

½ teaspoon baking soda

TO MAKE CRUMB MIXTURE: In a medium-size bowl, combine all ingredients; set them aside.

TO MAKE CAKE: Preheat the oven to 350°F. Lightly grease a 9-inch nonstick tube pan; set it aside. In a large mixing bowl, cream the butter alternative, brown sugar, and eggs until smooth and fluffy. Beat in the sour cream and vanilla. In a small bowl, sift together the flour, baking powder, and baking soda. Slowly add the flour mix to the batter, beating until smooth. (Use a rubber spatula to scrape down the sides and bottom of the bowl, and quickly mix again.) Pour half the batter into the tube pan; top evenly with ½ of the crumb mixture. Pour the remaining batter over the crumbs, spreading evenly with a rubber spatula. Top with the remaining crumb mixture. Bake 45 minutes. Cool for 30 minutes before serving.

Mary and Al Zappala on their wedding day, September 24, 1953.

A recent Thanksgiving with Mary and Al. Of course, Sour Cream Coffee Cake was on the menu!

Pumpkin Cheesecake

This dessert will make you a star! Given to me by my dear friend Frank, this cheescake has elevated me to star status in my home. It's great for the holidays or any time you want an exceptional treat.

NUTRITIONAL NOTE
Pumpkin is loaded with beta-carotene and vitamin E.

NUTRITION FACTS
(Per serving)
Calories: 260
Total Fat: 15 gms
Sodium: 298 mgs
Carbohydrates: 39 gms
Protein: 12 gms
Fiber: 5.1 gms

PREP TIME: 15-20 minutes   **COOK TIME:** 1 hour, 5 minutes   Serves 8

CRUST

1 10-ounce bag gingersnap cookies, crushed (about 2 cups)

½ cup chopped pecans

¼ cup natural buttery spread (such as Earth Balance or
    Smart Balance), melted

1 tablespoon Sucanat*

*Sucanat is an unrefined, unprocessed sugar that is a more healthful alternative to refined brown sugar.

FILLING

3 8-ounce packages reduced-fat cream cheese, softened

1 cup Sucanat

1 cup canned pumpkin

3 eggs

1 teaspoon vanilla

½ teaspoon cinnamon

¼ teaspoon nutmeg

¼ teaspoon allspice

Whole or chopped pecans for garnish

TO MAKE CRUST: Preheat the oven to 350°F. Lightly grease a 9-inch springform pan. Wrap the outside of the pan with foil. In a food processor, pulse together the cookies and pecans until they're finely ground. In a medium-size bowl, combine the cookie mixture with the melted butter alternative and the Sucanat; mix thoroughly. Press the crust mixture onto the bottom and 2 inches up the sides of the pan. Bake for 5 minutes. Remove the crust from the oven; set it aside. Keep the oven on.

TO MAKE FILLING: In a large mixing bowl, blend the cream cheese and Sucanat until smooth. Add the pumpkin, eggs, vanilla, cinnamon, nutmeg, and allspice; beat until smooth.

TO ASSEMBLE AND COOK: Pour the filling into the baked crust. Scrape the sides of the bowl with a rubber spatula to get all the filling. Bake the cheesecake until the center is set and the edges begin to crack, about 1 hour, 5 minutes. Remove the cake from the oven; cool for 20 minutes. Chill uncovered for 6 hours. Garnish with whole or chopped pecans.

Chocolate Torte

My family and friends say this decadent dessert reminds them of a brownie, only richer. Serve it with a scoop of fat-free vanilla frozen yogurt and some fresh raspberries, and you'll think you've died and gone to dessert heaven!

NUTRITIONAL NOTE

Sucanat is non-refined cane sugar that has not had the molasses removed from it like refined sugars, making it a more nutritious baking alternative.

NUTRITION FACTS

(Per serving)
Calories: 195
Total Fat: 10.5 gms
Sodium: 122 mgs
Carbohydrates: 19 gms
Protein: 7.3 gms
Fiber: 0 gms

PREP TIME: **25 minutes**   COOK TIME: **40-45 minutes**   Serves 8

---

2 4-ounce boxes Baker's all-natural sweet chocolate, or 8 ounces mildly
    sweet, dark chocolate chips

1 cup natural buttery spread (such as Earth Balance or Smart Balance)

5 eggs, separated

½ teaspoon vanilla

1½ cups Sucanat

Pinch of salt

¼ teaspoon cream of tartar

1 tablespoon powdered sugar, sifted

Preheat the oven to 350°F. Lightly grease a 9-inch springform pan; set it aside. In a medium-size bowl, combine the chocolate with the butter alternative. Set the bowl over a pot of simmering water and melt the chocolate mixture. (Make sure the top of the pot is a little smaller than the bowl size.) Remove the bowl from the heat; stir the mixture thoroughly. Set it aside. In a large mixing bowl, beat the egg yolks with the vanilla and Sucanat until they're thoroughly combined. In a separate medium-size mixing bowl, add the egg whites, pinch of salt, and cream of tartar. Beat the egg-white mixture on medium-high until it's foamy and stiff, about 4 minutes. Using a rubber spatula, fold in $^1/_3$ of the melted chocolate mixture to the egg yolk and Sucanat mixture; stir until smooth.

Fold in and stir another $^1/_3$ of the chocolate mixture, then the remaining $^1/_3$. In thirds, gently fold the egg whites into the chocolate batter, stirring until they're thoroughly combined. Pour the batter into the springform pan. Bake for 40-45 minutes or until firm and a toothpick inserted comes out clean. Cool at room temperature. Cover and chill 1 hour. Before serving, sprinkle lightly with powdered sugar.

Frosted Walnut Brownies

Few words are needed to describe these brownies! On a scale from 1 to 10, my family rates these a 10.5.

PREP TIME: **20-25 minutes** COOK TIME: **Approx. 35 minutes Serves 12-15**

NUTRITIONAL NOTE

Nutritionally, whole-wheat pastry flour and whole-wheat flour are the same, but pastry flour is much lighter and works very well in my dessert recipes. It's a complex carbohydrate, providing the main fuel for the body. If you can't find whole-wheat pastry flour, opt for unbleached white whole-wheat flour.

NUTRITION FACTS

(Per serving)

Calories: 400

Total Fat: 31 gms

Sodium: 83 mgs

Carbohydrates: 45 gms

Protein: 22 gms

Fiber: 3 gms

BROWNIES

3 1-ounce squares Baker's bittersweet baking chocolate

1 4-ounce box Baker's all-natural sweet-chocolate bar

1 cup natural buttery spread (such as Earth Balance or Smart Balance)

1 cup Sucanat*

4 eggs

1 cup whole-wheat pastry flour or unbleached white
    whole-wheat flour, sifted

1 cup walnuts, finely chopped

*Sucanat is an unrefined sweetener made from the whole sugar cane.

FROSTING

¼ cup Sucanat

3 tablespoons natural buttery spread (such as Earth Balance
    or Smart Balance)

¼ cup low-fat milk

1 cup powdered sugar

¼ cup mildly sweet dark chocolate chips

¼ cup walnuts, finely chopped for topping

TO MAKE BROWNIES: Preheat the oven to 375°F. Lightly grease an 11 x 7½-inch baking dish; set it aside. In a medium-size bowl, combine the bittersweet and all-natural-sweet chocolates with the butter alternative. Set the bowl over a pot of simmering water and melt the chocolate. (Make sure the top of the pot is a little smaller than the bowl size.) Remove the pot from the heat; stir the chocolate to combine. Let the mixture cool.

In a large mixing bowl, add the Sucanat, eggs, and flour; beat until smooth. Add the chocolate mixture and the walnuts; beat until thoroughly combined. Pour the batter into the baking dish. Bake for 30 minutes or until firm and a toothpick inserted comes out clean. Cool before frosting.

TO MAKE FROSTING: In a medium-size saucepan over medium heat, combine the Sucanat, butter alternative, low-fat milk, and powdered sugar; stir constantly for 1 minute. Stir in the chocolate chips until smooth. Spread the frosting evenly over the cooled brownies. Top with chopped walnuts.

Tiramisu

When translated from Italian, tiramisu means "pull" or "pick me up." You can thank the espresso in this recipe for that. My cousin Suzan shared this family favorite with me. It's a wonderfully satisfying Italian treat.

NUTRITIONAL NOTE
For a lower-fat version, substitute a high-quality, very fresh low-fat cream cheese for mascarpone cheese.

NUTRITION FACTS
(Per serving)
Calories: 200
Total Fat: 20 gms
Sodium: 94 mgs
Carbohydrates: 37 gms
Protein: 9 gms
Fiber: 2 gms

PREP TIME: **25-30 minutes**   COOK TIME: **5 minutes**   Serves 8-10

4 cups water

4 egg yolks

⅓ cup powdered sugar, sifted, plus 2 tablespoons powdered sugar, sifted, for topping

½ cup marsala wine

8-10 ounces mascarpone cheese

1½ cups whipping cream

1 teaspoon vanilla

2 packages ladyfinger cookies (about 40-42 cookies total)

1 cup espresso or strong coffee, slightly sweetened

1 tablespoon unsweetened, unprocessed cocoa, sifted

Bring the water to a boil in a medium-size saucepan over high heat. While the water is heating, in a medium-size stainless-steel mixing bowl, beat the egg yolks with the powdered sugar and marsala wine until combined. Set the bowl over the pot of boiling water. (Make sure the top of the pot is a little smaller than the bowl size.) Reduce the heat to medium. Whisk the egg mixture constantly until it's light and foamy, about 5 minutes. Set it aside to cool.

In a small mixing bowl, whip the mascarpone cheese until creamy (about 10 seconds). Beat the mascarpone into the egg mixture. In a medium-size bowl, whip the cream and vanilla until stiff. Fold the cream into the egg/cheese mixture, combining thoroughly. Arrange half the ladyfingers (about 20), cut-side down, on the bottom of a 13 x 7½-inch baking dish. With a tablespoon, drizzle just enough espresso or coffee over the ladyfingers to moisten them.

Spread half of the mascarpone/egg mixture over the layer of ladyfingers. Sprinkle 1 tablespoon of the powdered sugar over the top. Sprinkle ½ tablespoon of the sifted cocoa over the powdered sugar. Repeat layers once more. Refrigerate 2-3 hours before serving.

Key Lime Pie

You don't have to travel to Key West to get the best key lime pie. This sublime key lime provides a luscious, slightly tart taste experience — and you just have to travel to your kitchen for a slice.

PREP TIME: 30-35 minutes   COOK TIME: **10 minutes (for crust)**   Serves 6-8

CRUST

1¾ cups (about 14 ounces) whole-wheat honey graham cracker crumbs

¼ cup agave nectar

½ cup natural buttery spread (such as Earth Balance or
        Smart Balance), melted

FILLING

1 14-ounce can sweetened condensed milk

1 envelope plain gelatin

¼ cup water at room temperature

½ cup key lime juice (such as Nellie & Joe's Famous Key West Lime Juice)
        at room temperature

Zest of 1 lime

2 tablespoons honey

4 ounces cream cheese or reduced-fat cream cheese, softened

1 cup low-fat vanilla yogurt

TO MAKE CRUST: Preheat the oven to 350°F. Lightly grease a 9½-inch round Pyrex dish; set it aside. In a food processor, grind the cracker crumbs until fine. In a medium-size bowl, stir together the cracker crumbs, agave nectar, and melted butter alternative. Using your hands, mix the ingredients until they're thoroughly combined. Press the crumb mixture firmly on the bottom and up the sides of the Pyrex dish. Bake for 10 minutes. Remove the crust from the oven; let it cool. Turn off oven.

NUTRITIONAL NOTE
Whole-wheat flour is naturally healthier for you. A high-fiber food, it's also a good source of selenium and magnesium. Agave nectar, which has a low glycemic index, is a pure and tasty alternative to refined sugar. It's available as a light or dark syrup. For this recipe, the light agave, which is milder, works better.

NUTRITION FACTS
(Per serving)
Calories: 100
Total Fat: 5 gms
Sodium: 110 mgs
Carbohydrates: 17 gms
Protein: 6 gms
Fiber: 2 gms

TO MAKE FILLING: Bring the condensed milk to a gentle boil in a small saucepan over low heat, stirring occasionally. Remove the pan from the heat; let it cool. In a medium-size bowl, sprinkle the gelatin over the ¼ cup of water; let stand for 5-10 minutes. Set the bowl of gelatin over a pot of simmering water. (Make sure the top of the pot is a little smaller than the bowl size.) Stir a few seconds until the gelatin is dissolved. Remove the gelatin from the stove; whisk in the lime juice and lime zest. In a large mixing bowl, add the honey, cream cheese, and yogurt; beat until smooth. Add the gelatin mixture and the condensed milk to the large mixing bowl; whisk until thoroughly combined. Pour the filling into the baked pie crust. Chill 3 hours or until firm.

Crescent Cookies

Mom and her close friend Faye made these butter cookies for every holiday, every year, and no matter how many they made we always begged for more. Let that be fair warning: Double your recipe, double your pleasure.

PREP TIME: **25 minutes**   COOK TIME: **20 minutes**

Makes approx. 60 cookies

1 cup natural buttery spread (such as Earth Balance
    or Smart Balance), softened

1 cup powdered sugar, sifted, plus a little more for sprinkling

1 teaspoon vanilla

2½ cups whole-wheat pastry flour or unbleached white
    whole-wheat flour, sifted

1½ cup finely chopped walnuts

½ cup finely chopped pecans

Preheat the oven to 350°F. In a large mixing bowl, cream the butter alternative. Add 1 cup of the powdered sugar, a little at a time. Add the vanilla, then gradually add the flour and nuts alternately (start with flour and end with flour); mix thoroughly. Take a heaping teaspoon of dough and roll between your palms; place on nonstick cookie sheet and form into a crescent shape. Repeat to make approximately 60 cookies. (You'll need 2 large, nonstick cookie sheets.) Bake for 20 minutes. Cool on the cookie sheets for 15-20 minutes. Remove the cookies to a plate. Sprinkle them with powdered sugar.

NUTRITIONAL NOTE

Walnuts and pecans contain heart-healthy monounsaturated and polyunsaturated fats. Also, the fiber in these nuts may help lower cholesterol levels.

NUTRITION FACTS

(Per cookie)

Calories: 60

Total Fat: 4 gms

Sodium: 25 gms

Carbohydrates: 5.6 gms

Protein: 3 gms

Fiber: 2 gms

Mondel Bread

This recipe came from one of my mother's best friends, who made mondel bread during the Jewish holidays. She had us all "kvelling" over these treats. As kids, we ate them endlessly, dunking them into cold milk. I remember that the adults loved to dunk theirs in hot coffee, much like they did with the Italian cookie, biscotti. In fact, these cookies are very similar to biscotti.

NUTRITIONAL NOTE

Whole-wheat flour is naturally healthier for you. A high-fiber food, it's also a good source of selenium and magnesium, that are nutrients essential to good health. Unbleached white whole-wheat flour is high in fiber and has fewer carbohydrates than white flour.

NUTRITION FACTS

(Per 2 cookie serving)
Calories: 120
Total Fat: 3 gms
Sodium: 130 mgs
Carbohydrates: 23 gms
Protein: 2 gms
Fiber: 4 gms

PREP TIME: **15-20 minutes**   COOK TIME: **Approx. 55 minutes**

Makes approx. 40 cookies

---

3 eggs

1 cup Sucanat*

¾ cup canola oil

2¾ cups whole-wheat pastry flour or unbleached white
    whole-wheat flour, sifted

1 teaspoon baking powder, sifted

2 teaspoons vanilla

1 tablespoon flour for coating nuts

1 cup ground walnuts

*Sucanat is a natural sugar cane that is unrefined and unprocessed, making it a more healthful alternative to brown sugar.

Preheat the oven to 350°F. In a large mixing bowl, beat together the eggs, Sucanat, and canola oil. Add the sifted flour, baking powder, and vanilla to the egg mixture; combine thoroughly. In a small bowl, combine the 1 tablespoon of flour and the walnuts; mix to coat well. Stir the nut mixture into the egg-and-flour mixture. On a large nonstick cookie sheet, shape the dough into 6-inch loaves for smaller cookies, or 12-inch loaves for larger cookies. Bake for 35 minutes. Remove the loaves from the oven and cut them into ¾- to 1-inch-thick slices with a serrated knife. Return to oven for 18-20 minutes until they are lightly toasted. Cool for 20 minutes.

TIP: *You can use an electric mixer to start, but you may have to finish mixing with a large spoon, as the batter gets a bit sticky. Flour your hands before handling dough to prevent sticking.*

Dad's Favorite Pignoli Cookies

My dad's parents hailed from Sicily. They were quite a pair. While Grandpa made wine in the basement, Grandma was in the kitchen making pignolis, which are almond-flavored cookies with pine nuts. Pignoli is the Italian word for "pine nut," and in Italian households, pignolis are especially popular during the holidays, though Dad loves them year-round. With this recipe, you can enjoy an old family favorite anytime, one that's just as tasty today as it was years ago in Sicily.

NUTRITIONAL NOTE

Pine "nuts" are actually seeds, that come from pinecones. They're chock-full of vitamins A, C, and D, and contain monounsaturated fat, the "good" fat that, when eaten in moderation, can be part of a healthful diet.

NUTRITION FACTS

(Per cookie)
Calories: 149
Total Fat: 8.35 gms
Sodium: 56.5 mgs
Carbohydrates: 13.6 gms
Protein: 6.9 gms
Fiber: 3 gms

PREP TIME: **25-30 minutes**   COOK TIME: **20 minutes**

Makes approx. 30-35 cookies

12 ounces almond paste, crumbled

2 egg whites, plus 2 more egg whites for coating

½ cup light-brown sugar

1 cup powdered sugar, sifted

2 cups pignoli nuts (pine nuts)

Flour to dust hands to prevent sticking

Preheat the oven to 325°F. Lightly grease 3 medium-size nonstick cookie sheets. In a large mixing bowl, beat the crumbled almond paste, 2 egg whites, and brown sugar until combined. (Don't worry about the lumps, they will smooth out after you add the powdered sugar.) Slowly add the powdered sugar; beat until smooth. In a small bowl, add the remaining 2 egg whites, whisk until combined, and set aside. Spread the pine nuts on a flat plate.

Flour your hands to prevent sticking as you handle the dough. Shape the batter into 1-inch balls. Roll the balls in the egg whites, shaking off any excess. Then roll them in the pine nuts. Arrange the cookie balls 1 inch apart on the cookie sheets, pressing down lightly to flatten. Bake for 20 minutes or until golden brown. Cool for 30 minutes.

Mandarin Orange-Walnut and Sour Cream Jell-O

This age-old treat conjures up childhood memories of Mom at the stove, making a dessert that we always had room for. With this version, J-e-l-l-o spells joy, excellence, light, luscious, and outstanding!

PREP TIME: **5 minutes**	COOK TIME: **5 minutes**	Serves 4

1 cup water

1 3-ounce package orange Jell-O

1 cup low-fat sour cream

1 11-ounce can mandarin oranges in light syrup, drained

¼ cup chopped walnuts

Bring the water to a boil in a medium-size saucepan over high heat. Reduce the heat to medium. Add the Jell-O; stir until dissolved. Remove the pan from the heat. Add the sour cream; whisk a few seconds until thoroughly combined. Stir in the oranges and walnuts. Pour the mixture into 4 individual 10-ounce ramequins. Chill at least 1 hour, or until firm.

NUTRITIONAL NOTE

Mandarin oranges are a very good source of fiber and vitamins A and C.

NUTRITION FACTS

(Per serving)

Calories: 150

Total Fat: 10 gms

Sodium: 20 mgs

Carbohydrates: 18 gms

Protein: 4.5 gms

Fiber: 3.6 gms

Baked Apples

My family ate this nutritious dessert whenever we wanted a different take on apples. The nuts make a tasty addition, along with just a dollop of whipped topping.

NUTRITIONAL NOTE

Apples are one of the most nutritious fruits we can eat, and that includes the skin for its vitamins and fiber. Try to buy organic apples which contain less pesticides and other chemicals that apple skins are exposed to.

NUTRITION FACTS

(Per serving)

Calories: 175

Total Fat: 1.4 gms

Sodium: 188 mgs

Carbohydrates: 36 gms

Protein: 2 gms

Fiber: 5.1 gms

PREP TIME: 10-15 minutes	COOK TIME: 12 minutes	Serves 4

4 organic Red Delicious apples, washed, unpeeled, cored, and cut into
   ½-inch cubes

2 tablespoons natural buttery spread (such as Earth Balance
   or Smart Balance)

3 tablespoons honey

Pinch of nutmeg

2 teaspoons apple cider or apple juice

1 teaspoon cinnamon

Nonfat whipped topping (optional)

½ cup finely chopped walnuts or pecans, toasted*

*To toast the nuts, arrange them on a baking sheet and toast for 7-10 minutes at 350°F.

Preheat the oven to 350°F. Place the apple pieces in a 13 x 9-inch baking dish; set it aside. Melt the butter alternative in a small saucepan over low heat. Add the honey, nutmeg, apple cider or juice, and cinnamon. Stir constantly until the ingredients are thoroughly combined and are a toasty brown color. Pour the mixture over the apples, mixing thoroughly to coat. Bake for 12 minutes. Top the baked apples with the toasted nuts and a dollop of whipped topping. Serve warm.

TIP: *I love the 365 Everyday Value Real Dairy Nonfat Whipped Topping. It's delicious and lighter than traditional whipped toppings and contains no added sugar.*

Anytime Snacks

Blast in a Glass

Egg in a Basket

Veggie Sandwich

Blast in a Glass

This is a favorite of mine because it's as satisfying and delicious as a milk shake, and filled to the rim with ingredients that are good for you. Considering all of the nutrients you'll be consuming, this really is a blast in a glass. "Cheers!" to your health.

NUTRITIONAL NOTE

Flaxseed is rich in omega-3 fatty acids, essential for good health and glowing skin. Wheat germ is a good source of folic acid and fiber.

NUTRITION FACTS

(Per serving)
Calories: 260
Total Fat: 2.4 gms
Sodium: 102 mgs
Carbohydrates: 41.7 gms
Protein: 19.8 gms
Fiber: 4.8 gms

PREP TIME: **5 minutes**   Makes about 2, 8-ounce glasses

---

1 banana

6 fresh or frozen strawberries*

¼ cup fresh or frozen blueberries and/or raspberries*

½ cup low-fat or skim milk (or nondairy substitute such as
    rice or almond milk)

½ cup low-fat or nonfat plain or vanilla yogurt

1 scoop plain or vanilla-flavored whey protein powder

1 tablespoon ground flaxseed

1 tablespoon wheat germ

For an icy cold smoothie, use frozen fruit.

Mix all ingredients thoroughly in a blender for about 20 seconds. Pour into chilled glasses and drink up.

Egg in a Basket

You'll love this quick, all-in-one egg-and-toast dish for its taste and convenience. I love whole-grain breads, but you can also make this with a slice of fresh Italian bread.

PREP TIME: **5 minutes**	COOK TIME: **5 minutes**	Serves 1

Canola oil nonstick spray

1 teaspoon natural buttery spread (such as Earth Balance or Smart Balance)

1 slice whole-grain or whole-wheat bread

1 egg

Salt and pepper to taste

Coat a small skillet with nonstick spray. Place the skillet over medium heat for 1 minute. Spread the butter alternative on one side of the bread. Cut a small, round hole in the middle of the bread slice, just big enough to hold an egg yolk. Place the bread buttered-side down in the pan. Break the egg gently into the hole in the bread. Cook for 2 minutes or until the bottom side of the bread turns golden brown. Using a plastic spatula, scoop the bread/egg up out of the skillet and gently turn it over. Cook for another 1-2 minutes or until bottom side of bread is a golden brown. Sprinkle the bread/egg with salt and pepper to taste. Serve immediately.

NUTRITIONAL NOTE

Eggs have been maligned over the years, but recent studies have found that eggs are one of the most nutritious foods available. In fact, studies show that people who eat two eggs a day as part of a low-fat diet do not show signs of increased blood cholesterol levels. (Diabetics and people with cholesterol concerns are an exception and should check with their doctor.) Eggs are high in protein and various B vitamins and are also a rich source of vitamin D.

NUTRITION FACTS

(Per serving)

Calories: 180

Total Fat: 6 gms

Sodium: 273 mgs

Carbohydrates: 18.6 gms

Protein: 9.3 gms

Fiber: 2 gms

Veggie Sandwich

Enjoy this especially tasty sandwich anytime you're in the mood for a nibble or a nosh. This easy-to-make snack is low in fat and calories, yet still tastes delicious.

PREP TIME: **5 minutes**   COOK TIME: **7 minutes for a hot sandwich**

Serves 1

Light mayonnaise and/or mustard

2 slices whole-grain bread

2 slices roasted turkey

2 slices reduced-fat Swiss cheese (such as Jarlsberg Lite)

4 slices ripe Roma tomato

4 slices avocado

Handful of broccoli or alfalfa sprouts

Salt and pepper to taste

FOR COLD SANDWICH: Spread some mayonnaise and/or mustard on one slice of bread. Layer the bread with roasted turkey slices, cheese, tomato, avocado, sprouts, and salt and pepper to taste. Top with the remaining bread slice. Cut the sandwich in half. Serve with fresh fruit and whole-grain chips.

FOR HOT SANDWICH: Set toaster oven temperature on toast/broil. Spread mayonnaise and/or mustard on one slice of bread. Layer the bread with roasted turkey slices, cheese, and tomato. Place the sandwich in the toaster oven; set on broil for 7 minutes. After 4 minutes, place remaining bread slice in oven beside the first slice. When done, remove both slices from the oven. Add the avocado and sprouts, season with salt and pepper, and top with the remaining bread slice. Cut the sandwich in half and serve.

NUTRITIONAL NOTE

Whole grains are part of a healthful diet, as are tomatoes and avocado. Broccoli sprouts are rich in fiber and vitamins C, E, and A, and are loaded with minerals, especially potassium.

NUTRITION FACTS

(Per serving)

Calories: 238

Total Fat: 13 gms

Sodium: 262 mgs

Carbohydrates: 32 gms

Protein: 18 gms

Fiber: 7 gms

Healthier Alternatives

ALL-NATURAL MEATS AND POULTRY — These meats contain no antibiotics, no added hormones, and no animal by-products. However, a small amount of pesticides, as approved by the FDA, can be used — about the same amount used on nonorganic fruits and vegetables.

EXTRA-VIRGIN OLIVE OIL — This is considered the best and the least-processed oil. It contains no additives or preservatives. Extra-virgin olive oil is typically produced from the first pressing of olives, so it is the purest and least acidic, making it the best tasting of the olive oils. Also look for "cold pressed" on the label; that means the oil is extracted using no heat, which can destroy the healthful antioxidants found in olive oil, namely vitamin E.

NATURAL BUTTERY SPREADS — Avoiding trans fats to maintain good health is a must. Many butters and margarines contain partially hydrogenated oils (trans fats), which over time may contribute to heart disease. That's why I use butter alternatives such as Earth Balance and Smart Balance. Both are trans fat free, and contain omega-3 fatty acids, the "good" fats essential for optimum health.

ORGANIC FRUITS AND VEGETABLES — These fruits and vegetables are grown using no pesticides, although most experts agree that the amount of pesticides found on conventional produce poses very little health risk. Even so, I try to go organic when I can, particularly when purchasing produce that's usually eaten with the skin on, such as apples, grapes, peaches, bell peppers, and zucchini. Organic products are usually a bit more expensive, so it's a good idea to look for specials and store-brand organic items, which are often less expensive than name-brand items.

ORGANIC MEATS AND POULTRY — These meats and poultry contain no antibiotics, no added hormones, no animal by-products, and no pesticides. Organic products are also environmentally friendly since organic farming practices help to reduce pollution and conserve water and soil. Animals from organic farms are also treated more humanely.

SUGARS — It's important to watch your sugar intake, but unrefined, unprocessed raw sugars are always the healthier choice. In most of my recipes, I use all unrefined raw sugars which contain minerals and nutrients that are stripped from refined white sugar. Sucanat is one of my favorites and can be used in most of my dessert recipes. It's pure dried cane juice, and ranks the highest in nutritional value, as it contains a smaller proportion of sucrose than white cane sugar.

365 EVERYDAY VALUE REAL DAIRY NONFAT WHIPPED TOPPING — This is a guiltless pleasure that tastes like regular whipped cream, but it has no added sugar. It can be found online and at Whole Foods Markets.

UNCURED MEATS — These meats contain no additives or nitrates, a preservative that is also used to set color in foods.

WHOLE GRAINS — Whole-wheat pastas, breads, and crackers are excellent sources of complex carbohydrates which provide the main fuel for the body. Since they haven't had their bran and germ removed, they're much higher in dietary fiber and other healthful nutrients than refined grains such as white breads and pastas.

WHOLE-WHEAT PASTRY FLOUR — Great for baking. This healthful and wholesome flour is an alternative to white flour, which is stripped of most of its nutrients. Whole grains provide essential dietary fiber, vitamins, and minerals.

UNBLEACHED WHITE WHOLE-WHEAT FLOUR — A lighter and milder whole-wheat flour. Good for baking some cakes, cookies, and breads.

Kitchen Keepers

Essential tools for making your cooking experience nearly effortless.

Baking Sheets and Dishes
(Small/Medium/Large)

Blender

Box Grater

Cake Pans

Can Opener

Casserole Dishes

Chef's Knife

Colander

Cookie Sheets

Crock-Pot

Cutting Boards

Digital Scale

Electric Mixer

Food Processor

Grater/Zester

Immersion Blender

Kitchen Scissors

Ladle

Liquid Measuring Cups

Measuring Spoons

Meat Tenderizer

Meat Thermometer

Metal Whisk

Mixing Bowls
(Small/Medium/Large)

Oven Mitts

Paring Knife

Pastry Brush

Pyrex Dishes/Bowls

Ramequins

Rubber Spatula

Serrated Knife

Serving Bowls

Sifter

Skillets (Small/Medium/
Large/Extra-Large), Oven-Safe

Slotted Spoon

Solid Measuring Cups

Spaghetti Server

Spatula or Turner

Spice Rack

Spoon Rest

Springform Pan

Stainless-Steel Saucepans
(Small/Medium/Large/Extra-
Large), with Lids

Stainless-Steel Sauce Pots
(Small/Medium/Large/Extra-
Large), with Lids

Stainless-Steel Skimmer
or Strainer

Steamer

Stirring Spoons

Toaster Oven

Tongs

Tube Pan

Vegetable Brush

Vegetable Peeler

Wooden Spoons

Acknowledgments

I would like to thank several people for jumping on this fast-moving train with me and going for a ride I know I'll never forget. I thank Chef Matthew Babbage for helping to test my recipes and making sure they were the very best they could be. To Betty Barlow, April Lisante, and Barbara Sperrazza, thank you for contributing your time and talents to make this book first-rate. To Mary Anne Claro, Pat Gieder, and Zina Minz, I thank you for your thoughtful guidance and unwavering encouragement. To Christina Pirello, you've been a source of great inspiration to me for as long as I've known you. Thank you for being there when I needed you.

I also want to thank my loving husband, Steve, and my beautiful daughter, Natalya, for understanding why I spent nearly every hour of the day and night for months at the computer, that is, when I wasn't cooking. (At least they were able to enjoy the fruits of my labor.) I extend a heartfelt thanks to my wonderful son, Brad, who, along with his buddies, planted the seed for this book, imploring me to write about my recipes so they, too, could learn to cook. (The jury is still out on that one.)

I would be remiss if I didn't extend my sincere gratitude to my publisher, Rod Colvin at Addicus Books. Your keen awareness of the process, your attention to detail, and your faith in me are appreciated more than you know. You have been my mentor and my guiding light.

Finally, a great big hug to my always-supportive father, Albert, and brother, Ron, a great cook in his own right, who rounded up some of Mom's "lost" recipes and made sure they made their way to me. *My Italian Kitchen* could not have been as complete without your help.

Recipe Index

W

Z

About the Author

Janet Zappala is an award-winning television news journalist. She has won six Emmy awards and garnered thirteen Emmy nominations for her work at TV stations in cities across the country, including Honolulu, San Diego, Los Angeles, Denver, and Philadelphia. She is also the recipient of a Golden Mike award for her profile on Mel Blanc, "The Man of a Thousand Voices," and she received a first-place Associated Press award for her feature reporting.

Named one of the "Best in the Business" by the *Washington Journalism Review*, Janet has anchored television newscasts in Denver, Los Angeles, and Philadelphia. She served as host of "All About You," a consumer-health program on the Comcast Network. She also co-hosted a syndicated news and entertainment magazine show for Fox Television. Janet has interviewed hundreds of newsmakers, ranging from U.S. presidents to celebrities. She holds a master of arts degree in liberal studies from Villanova University and an undergraduate degree in journalism. She is also a certified nutritional consultant. Janet may be reached through her Web site: **www.janetzappala.com.**

To order copies of

My Italian Kitchen...